ROYALTY IN VOGUE

ROYALTY IN VOGUE

JOSEPHINE ROSS

Designed by Louise Brody

CHATTO & WINDUS

LONDON

Published in 1989 by
Chatto & Windus Ltd
30 Bedford Square
London WC1B 3SG

A CIP catalogue record for this book is available from
the British Library.

ISBN 0 7011 3381 3

Printed in Great Britain by
Butler & Tanner, Frome, Somerset

Page 1 State procession 1935 *Pagès*
Page 2 Princess Elizabeth with Prince Charles 1950 *Beaton*
Cartouches on *page 5* and throughout drawn by Rex Whistler

Contents

Introduction 6

Fanfare and Ceremony 26

Royal Weddings 42

Family Life 70

The Windsor Story 94

In War and Peace 114

Abroad and At Home 132

Royal Style 162

Family Tree 204

Index 206

Acknowledgements 208

INTRODUCTION

The American-born Lady Decies,
in Court dress

King George V
at the Richmond Horse Show

When the American publisher Condé Nast acquired *Vogue*, in 1909, it was a small weekly gazette, dedicated to 'Society, fashion and the ceremonial side of life.' Published in New York, it had been founded seventeen years before with the backing of such prominent figures as Cornelius Vanderbilt and Mrs Stuyvesant Fish; in the 1890s the early issues had reflected their world, with society news and photographs, fashion articles and reviews of the arts, as well as regular reports from London and Paris. Under Condé Nast's direction, 'a bigger, a better and a still more attractive *Vogue*' was announced, to be published fortnightly; and in the years that followed, the little society gazette was to become the most famous and successful fashion magazine of the 20th century. Yet the original aims remained. Besides fashionable living, 'the ceremonial side of life' was of unfailing interest to *Vogue*'s readers; they were, or aspired to be, of the affluent groups who might present a daughter at Court, order a dress from a Royal designer, meet a Prince at a house-party, or attend a Coronation. Royalty was always in *Vogue*; and today the past issues since 1909 have come to represent an unrivalled archive of informed and sophisticated royal reporting.

A new era was about to begin when Nast took over *Vogue*. In Britain, the reign of Queen Victoria's popular son Edward VII was drawing to a close, and the map of royal Europe was soon to be re-drawn amid the upheavals of the First World War. 'That the old order which has obtained during the past ten years will give place to the new, is only to be expected', *Vogue* wrote with unconscious prophecy in May 1911, as London prepared for the Coronation of the new King and Queen. The same issue carried photographs of the children of the Czar of Russia, with the caption, 'The Czarevitch is the most guarded child in Europe'; but *Vogue*'s chief concern, in that Coronation year, was that King George V and his dutiful consort, Queen Mary, might set a dull and unfashionable tone for London society. Early hours and 'somewhat strict lines of conduct' at Court were threatened; the

Queen was said to dress badly, in 'atrocious modes of mid-Victorian vintage'; and – most disappointing to *Vogue*'s readers – there were suggestions that Americans might no longer be as welcome in Court circles as they had been under the cosmopolitan Edward VII. The English themselves, *Vogue*'s *As Seen By Him* column asserted, 'do not care very much . . . as a personal matter, whether George and Mary are crowned or not.'

By 1914, however, the editorial attitude had changed. As memories of Edwardian glamour faded, stately dignity began to be seen as the proper mode for royalty. The image of a stout sovereign in loud check tweeds, surrounded by a royal 'fast set' of bankers and actresses, was replaced in *Vogue*'s pages by the short, upright, sober figure of George V – driving in the Gold Coach to the State Opening of Parliament (a sight 'almost barbaric in its splendour'), presenting prizes at the Richmond Horse Show, or riding in Rotten Row with his daughter. Queen Mary, readers were reassured, showed 'a great appreciation for the American element in London society'. She might lack the exquisite beauty of Edward VII's widow, Queen Alexandra; and she could never have been described as 'the best-dressed Queen of Europe', as was Queen Ena of Spain, whose clothes were 'modelled in the famous ateliers of Paris'; but she was found to have a magnificence which transcended fashion. For her appearance at one of the last Courts before the Great War, *Vogue* noted with awe: 'The Queen wore a gown of blue and silver brocade, and from her shoulders hung a diaphanous train of Honiton lace. On her corsage blazed the great African diamond, beneath which she wore the ribbon of the Garter.'

The beginning of the First World War – 'the greatest international conflict in history' – was marked in the issue of October 1, 1914, by a page of photographs of the royal protagonists: the allies Czar Nicholas II of all the Russias and King George V of Great Britain, and their common enemy and cousin, Kaiser William II of Germany. *Vogue* at first maintained a neutral stance, even publishing a picture of the smiling Kaiser with his grandson, 'a future kaiser', in a feature on the war-work of the Czar's pretty daughters (who were soon to die in the Russian Revolution). In 1916, however – a year before America entered the War – the magazine established close ties with Great Britain, when Condé Nast founded the first separate, overseas

Children of the Czar:
above Alexis, *below* Anastasia

7

Princess Patricia
in going-away clothes

edition, in London. Despite, or perhaps in part because of, wartime conditions, British *Vogue* flourished – to be followed, in the early 1920s, by French *Vogue*. Though each edition would cover 'society, fashion and the ceremonial side of life' from its own viewpoint, and in its own style, after 1916 *Vogue*'s enthusiasm for British royalty was assured.

In a pre-war article on society's changing ways, *Vogue* had observed, 'The King and Queen . . . do not approve of intermarriage with blood relatives or with the effete progeny of European royalty.' The aftermath of the War saw a series of royal weddings in London which seemed to bear out that statement. 'Even a princess may prefer romance to royalty', American *Vogue* announced in the spring of 1919, explaining that King George V's artistic cousin, Princess Patricia of Connaught (a granddaughter of Queen Victoria), had, 'with characteristic impulse and unconventionality', not only married a commoner, the Hon Alexander Ramsay, but had voluntarily 'discarded her title, with its accompanying prerogatives and immunities, to become Lady Victoria Ramsay.' As Lady Victoria, however, the former 'Princess Pat' was married in royal style, setting a new trend by choosing the Gothic magnificence of Westminster Abbey, where no royal wedding had taken place for many years.

Three years later, in late February, 1922, British *Vogue* published its first special 'Royal Wedding Number' for the marriage of King George V and Queen Mary's only daughter, the pretty, retiring Princess Mary. As a 'gesture of friendliness to the women of the Empire', *Vogue* recorded, 'The Queen and Princess Mary have waived their well-known dislike of unnecessary publicity . . . and allowed details of Princess Mary's trousseau to be made public.' Along with photographs of the bride and her bridegroom, the distinguished Viscount Lascelles, the silver-covered issue carried pages of sketches of 'becoming hats', crêpe de Chine afternoon frocks and delicately-embroidered evening gowns, chosen by 'the Nation's bride'. Details of the wedding-dress itself were released in time for a drawing to appear in the following issue, which contained a full account of the wedding and the 'magnificent attire' of the guests. The bride, in the unvarying language of royal weddings, was 'a Fairy Princess', with glass coach and pearl-embroidered dress; Queen Mary, 'in royal and stately beauty', wore lamé and velvet, topped by a golden toque; while Edward VII's widow, the ever-lovely Queen Alexandra, 'was in soft orchid velvet, with a diadem-like toque of iridescent sequins'. Ceremonial, rather than fashion, still dictated royal dress.

In the following year, another special issue of *Vogue* appeared, to mark what was – unknown to any at the time – to be one of the most significant royal occasions of the century: the marriage of the King and Queen's second son, the Duke of York, and the Lady Elizabeth Bowes-Lyon, daughter of the Earl of Strathmore. Lady Elizabeth had already appeared in *Vogue*, in a charming debutante photograph taken at a window, and in an informal house-party snapshot, at her father's Scottish seat, Glamis Castle. Her marriage to the King's dignified, naval-officer son, who had seen wartime action at the Battle of Jutland, was to prove popular; and *Vogue*'s 'Royal Wedding Number' included, along with full-page photographs of the bride and groom, and the now-customary trousseau sketches, a poem addressed to the 'princely-chosen maid', and specially-commissioned articles on bridal themes, by Aldous Huxley and Osbert Sitwell. Long before their destiny became known, the future King George VI and Queen Elizabeth were regarded with particular affection by the media, *Vogue* included.

'This is the age when new thought has been adding notes to the Court Guide', *Vogue* wrote in 1924. Queens, such as the beautiful Queen of Spain, could now be seen dining in London in public restaurants; and 'the daughters of royalty', with their 'short hair and short skirts', were 'as pretty and modish as the girls one sees on magazine covers'. Popular as King George and Queen Mary had become, public attention in the 1920s was increasingly focused on the younger royal generation, who were shaking off some of the old conventions to travel, dance and dress more like their fashionable contemporaries. The newly-

Princess Mary's wedding

Queen Mary with the Duke and Duchess of York
Pacific and Atlantic

Above The Mountbattens
Pictorial Press
Below At the Derby: the Prince of
Wales, the Duke of York and the Duke
of Gloucester *Alfieri*

The Prince of Wales

married York and Lascelles couples were often in *Vogue*, seen at the Derby, Goodwood, or the Hendon Aerial Pageant; while their dashing second cousin Lord Louis Mountbatten and his chic wife Edwina were mentioned frequently – crossing the Atlantic on ocean liners, or decorating their Park Lane apartment. The King's unmarried sons had differing tastes and social lives: the youngest, Prince George (the Duke of Kent), was elegant and artistic, with a liking for music and the theatre, while his elder brother Prince Henry (the Duke of Gloucester), was a good-looking, typically English sportsman and army officer, fond of country life, polo and hunting. All, however, were outshone in glamour by the heir to the throne, the handsome and charming Edward, Prince of Wales.

Early photographs of the Prince of Wales in *Vogue* had shown him as a somewhat wistful, fair-haired boy, decked in uniforms and orders. As early as 1913 (when he was just 19), *Vogue* had speculated as to whom he might marry, mentioning 'the stumbling-block of religion', which would rule out any Catholic princess, and suggesting one of the 'young and charming Russian princesses' as a solution. By the 1920s, however, it was apparent that the Prince had a mind – and a personality – of his own. On tours of the Empire, and visits to Europe and the United States, he displayed a relaxed, informal charm which, coupled with his extreme good looks, won him almost film-star status with the Press and the public. In Britain he was adored. He hunted with the Quorn, played polo and steeplechased; dined at Ciro's in Paris and danced at the Embassy Club in London; set fashions in dress by wearing plus-fours, Prince of Wales checks, Fair Isle sweaters and Breton berets. And he earned widespread approval with his expressions of sympathy for the unemployed. 'When will the Prince of Wales choose a bride, is always a preliminary query of the season', *Vogue* wrote in 1925. Ten years later the question remained – officially – unanswered.

Royal domesticity, meanwhile, was represented in *Vogue* by the Duke and Duchess of York and their two enchanting daughters, the Princesses Elizabeth and Margaret Rose. A series of studies by the photographer Marcus Adams marked the progress of the 'little Princesses', from babies, seen with their parents, or held by a stiff but fond Queen Mary, to grave small girls in party dresses. According to *Vogue*, the Duchess's dictum,

'I want her to be a frilly baby', had been taken up by nannies throughout Mayfair at the time of Princess Elizabeth's birth; and since then the 'York Nursery' had continued to lead young fashions – for high waists and coral necklaces, kilts with Shetland jumpers, and 'the sturdy little coats, the woollies and the scarfs that are so essentially of the style of these two Princesses'. It was a style which has persisted, with variations, down the generations of royal children.

For the epitome of feminine fashion and elegance, *Vogue* could look, after 1934, to a beautiful new member of the royal family – the Duke of Kent's bride, Princess Marina of Greece. Of mixed Greek and Russian descent, she had spent much of her youth in exile (partly in Paris), and had grown up with artistic tastes, immaculate dress sense, and a charming personality. The 'Royal Wedding Number' of November 28, 1934, broke new ground in *Vogue*, showing for the first time a royal princess photographed by a great fashion photographer: Horst. 'Princess Marina posed specially in the *Vogue* Studio for Mr Horst, who took all these lovely pictures', ran the caption to a series of classic images of the future Duchess, wearing clothes by the English-born couturier Molyneux, and posing with assured grace. Sketches of the Molyneux trousseau and wedding-dress followed, as well as a specially-commissioned portrait of the Duchess by *Vogue*'s fashion-artist Eric; there were photographs of the Kents' town-house, and details of the wedding-presents, from jewellers such as Cartier and Boucheron, and the decorators Syrie Maugham and Sibyl Colefax. It was, as *Vogue* pointed out, 'the first all-royal wedding of a king's son in England since 1795'; but the new Duke and Duchess of Kent possessed an entirely contemporary glamour.

There was another royal wedding a year later, when Prince Henry, the Duke of Gloucester, married Lady Alice Montagu-Douglas-Scott, daughter of the Duke of Buccleuch. This time, *Vogue*'s engagement picture of the bride was by Cecil Beaton. A regular contributor to *Vogue* for almost a decade, Beaton had first become known for his little drawings of society figures, and articles on such topics as 'The Fun of Dressing-Up'; but with the encouragement of Condé Nast he had rapidly emerged as one of the major portrait and fashion photographers of the age. His photograph of Lady Alice (a beautiful, outdoor-loving Scots-

The Little Princesses *Fox*

The Duke and Duchess of Kent *Beaton*

11

Beaton sketching
the future Duchess of Gloucester

King George V *Howard Coster*

woman), showed her in classic pose, reminiscent of Horst's studies of Princess Marina; and a sketch of the sitting accompanied its publication.

The dominating royal event of 1935, however, was the Silver Jubilee of King George V. Twenty-five years before, relatively small crowds had turned out to hail his Coronation; but the Jubilee summer was marked by a wave of joyous celebrations throughout the kingdom and empire. British *Vogue* published a special 'Jubilee Issue', with painted cover and gold-bordered photograph of the King, and suggested that readers might keep it as a reminder of 'these wonderful days when the London scene has been the dazzling envy of the world'. American *Vogue* carried a long article by a favourite contributor, John McMullin, who joined Elsa Schiaparelli's party at a hotel window, on May 6, to watch the royal procession pass on its way to the service of blessing in St Paul's Cathedral. He described a London of decorated balconies, flags, crowds, singing and excitement; he described the great procession as it passed – Princess Marina 'a dream in pale grey with a huge grey straw cartwheel hat', the Duchess of York 'very proud and sweet' – and King George and Queen Mary, 'those two wonderful human beings ... in their scarlet-lined gilded landau'; he described, too, the extraordinary, moving scene when the crowds in Pall Mall and St James's stood bareheaded or knelt to join in the prayers being broadcast over loudspeakers from St Paul's. 'It was thrilling, thrilling, thrilling.' That night, 'Buckingham Palace stood out white against the night, save when the King and Queen stepped onto the balcony, when the floodlighting was stopped and a spotlight thrown on them.' As the great showman C. B. Cochran observed to

McMullin, while watching the procession, it was 'as good as the best theatrical production'.

The glow of the Jubilee had not yet faded when the world learned of the King's final illness. *Vogue*'s issue of February 5, 1936, paid tribute to him on his death, saying truly, 'When thrones were falling on every hand beneath the stress of these times, he left the British monarchy more secure in the affection of its people and higher in the admiration of the world than ever before.' With the profound mourning for King George V, however, went excitement at the prospect of a glamorous new age – the reign of Edward VIII. 'Our thoughts turn with confidence to the happy times ahead', Seymour Leslie wrote in *Vogue*. 'New precedents are probable...' There was just one veiled hint in the article: 'Already one can fairly anticipate a desire that Americans ... should visit London this summer of 1936.' Those who moved in royal circles were already aware that one American, in particular, would feature in the new reign. Yet few could have guessed at the nature of the precedent which was about to be set.

Mrs Simpson, photographed and drawn for *Vogue* by Beaton

Since the early 30s, the name of Mrs Simpson had appeared more than once in *Vogue*. A chic, charming divorcée, born in Baltimore, she had come to London with her second husband, Ernest Simpson, and had become well-known in smart society. British *Vogue* quoted her ideas for cocktail snacks, and praised her dress-sense; American *Vogue* published a full-page photograph of her by Cecil Beaton. What the British media did not mention was her growing involvement with the man who was to become King of England. By 1936, however, the foreign press was agog. A close relationship between the king and a married woman was scandal enough; but when it became apparent that Edward VIII – who as monarch and Head of the Church of England was expressly debarred from marriage with a divorced woman – intended to marry Mrs Simpson, the stability of the Crown itself seemed threatened. A constitutional crisis loomed.

Throughout the eleven months of the reign, British *Vogue* made no reference to the affair. For American *Vogue*, however, the fact that a stylish and interesting American woman was closely involved with the King of England could not be ignored – especially since John McMullin was a friend of Wallis Simpson, and was therefore in touch with the historic events as they

King George VI and Queen Elizabeth
Wide World

Pierre Roy's Surrealist
Coronation issue cover

happened. Eventually it was arranged that Cecil Beaton should be given an exclusive sitting with Mrs Simpson; and two of the resulting pastel drawings appeared in American – though not British – *Vogue* in February, 1937, together with Beaton's impressions of the sitter. ('Her taste in clothes shows always a preference for bold simplicity, and her jewellery, especially for day, is extremely modern, though . . . the bracelet of little crosses is a surprise.') By then, however, the short reign of King Edward VIII had ended. Unable, as king, to marry the woman he loved, he had finally abdicated on December 11, 1936. 'After a nightmare of ten black days that seemed like an operation with incomplete anaesthesia – punctured by telephone calls, mad rumours, sudden fears, silent parties, deserted shops and distracted playgoers – the abdication of Edward VIII passed into history', Seymour Leslie wrote in American *Vogue*. The ex-king now had a new title, The Duke of Windsor; and his younger brother, the upright, responsible Duke of York, had become King George VI.

After the national crisis, it seemed important to stress the stability – and splendour – of the new reign. 'Paradoxically,' *Vogue* wrote, 'we are in for a much more brilliant Coronation under the new regime – because with a Queen the ceremony is complete.' *Vogue* was now full of royal features: reports on the preparations for the Coronation, articles on the King and Queen, accounts of the upbringing of Princess Elizabeth as heir to the throne. 'One thing is recognised that has never been acknowledged before in the schooling of an English Queen', a contributor wrote, 'that whatever state awaits her she has a right to be happy as a child.' The happy family life of the new monarchs was emphasised, as were their very British tastes – for Scottish holidays, gardening and shooting; for simple food and good music. At the same time, the details of royal magnificence and tradition were dwelt on, from the Coronation ritual to the robes of the peeresses. ('The quantities of each increase with rank until finally 4 rows of ermine, 5 inches of miniver, 6 feet of train distinguish a duchess from a mere baroness.') The Coronation Issue of April 28, 1937, combined old and new elements: the main article, 'Coronation Day', was by Sacheverell Sitwell, with illustrations by Rex Whistler, while the cover was the work of the Surrealist, Pierre Roy.

Just weeks after the Coronation, on June 3, 1937, the marriage of the Duke and Duchess of Windsor took place quietly, in France. Cecil Beaton not only took the official wedding-pictures, and wrote about the occasion for American *Vogue*, he was also given an exclusive sitting with Mrs Simpson shortly before, at which she wore clothes from her trousseau, by Mainbocher. Subsequent issues showed the Duchess shopping in Paris and being photographed, in her suite at the Hotel Meurice, by Horst; in the following year there was a feature on the Windsors at their new house, La Cröe, in Antibes. The fabulous lives of the Duke and Duchess of Windsor – their clothes, houses and personal style – continued to fascinate the public, especially in France (their home), and America; and American *Vogue* was to provide privileged glimpses of their world, up until the late 1960s.

After their Coronation, the new King George VI and Queen Elizabeth had begun an arduous round of public duties. 'They visit slums, hospitals, welfare centres, exhibitions, trade fairs, industrial centres . . . and the rest, while receiving bouquets and the Freedom of cities with tireless enthusiasm', the novelist Lesley Blanch (then on *Vogue*'s staff) wrote in 1939, reviewing the first two years on the throne of 'this hard-working, gallant and charming couple'. Against a background of mounting tensions in Europe, the King and Queen were called upon not only to strengthen national unity and morale, but also to reaffirm Britain's overseas friendships; and in 1938 and 1939 they undertook major foreign tours, to France, Canada and the United States. 'The American press will surely ferret out facts such as the Queen's skill with gun and rod . . . (and) that the King enjoys detective fiction', *Vogue* wrote. The royal image had never seemed more important.

For the fashion-conscious French, the Queen appeared in a ravishing new wardrobe, by Norman Hartnell, which for once disarmed the critics of British style. Based on the theme of white, with long, flowing lines for day, it included a group of gala dresses which, in *Vogue*'s words, 'launched the second crinoline fashion in all its billowing glory'. This romantically feminine image, redolent of the paintings of Winterhalter, was to provide the key to the series of classic photographs of Queen Elizabeth which Cecil Beaton took, from 1939 onwards. They showed the Queen as an almost ethereal figure, drifting in a cloud of tulle or

The Duke and Duchess of Windsor, on their wedding day *Beaton*

The King and Queen with Princess Elizabeth
British Press Combine

15

Wartime duties

Opposite Queen Elizabeth, 'an enchanting, almost fairy-story figure'
Beaton

The Royal Family at Windsor *Beaton*

poised amidst the magnificent interiors of Buckingham Palace – where the 'marble columns, ornate plasterwork, crystal chandeliers and ... acres of Savonnerie carpets' created perfect Beaton backgrounds. Describing his first sitting with the Queen in a 1953 article for *Vogue*, Beaton recalled, 'Wherever we went in the Palace ... the scene was dominated by the enchanting, almost fairy-story figure in her sparkles and spangles.' Posing in the gardens, in 'lacy day-dress and picture hat', the Queen remarked that the rose-red sunset sky often made Piccadilly look as if it were on fire. 'Before the pictures that were taken that afternoon could be released for publication,' Beaton wrote, 'the skies of London were red with the fires of war.'

Some of the most memorable images of the Second World War, from the London Blitz to the Burma Front, were to be created by Cecil Beaton himself, as an official photographer. He continued to photograph royalty, however; and many of the resulting portraits appeared in *Vogue*, accompanying features on the Royal Family in wartime. The Duchess of Kent, as 'head of navy women', was seen in WRNS uniform aboard a speeding motor-launch; the ultra-chic Edwina Mountbatten, busy with Red Cross and St John's Ambulance duties, now appeared in *Vogue* in 'the severe, dark blue St John uniform', only posing once in an evening dress, decked with lace, to support a fund-raising exhibition of antique lace sponsored by the Queen and Queen Mary. The 'feminine spiritedness' advocated in *Vogue* was exemplified, above all, by Queen Elizabeth, as she visited the blitzed East End, or – in another of Beaton's enduring images – cheerfully surveyed the bomb-damage at Buckingham Palace, with the King. She toured hospitals, reviewed troops and comforted casualties, yet still found time to visit picture galleries and take the Princesses to concerts – 'retaining and fostering ... culture, beauty and tradition', *Vogue* wrote. 'She is to the nation what more women should be to their families.'

As the war drew to an end, Princess Elizabeth became the subject of increasing public interest, as the heir-presumptive to the throne. She was often photographed by Beaton, in now-famous 'conversation piece' studies with the Queen and Princess Margaret, at Buckingham Palace, or amidst the 'sombre magnificence' of Windsor Castle; one portrait, at sixteen, showed her as honorary Colonel of the Grenadier Guards, with the regimental

Prince Philip *Baron*

The Royal Wedding *Baron*

insignia in her cap. As *Vogue* put it, she had acquired a 'breadth of social instinct' through meeting diplomats and airmen, cabinet ministers and musicians; hers was a world of receptions for the Allies, 'tours of aerodromes and centres of industry', and 'close contact with her contemporaries' in the Girl Guides and the A.T.S. The old royal life of levées and gilded isolation had gone for ever.

The wedding of the Princess Elizabeth to the former Lt Philip Mountbatten, in November 1947, was to lift the spirits of a post-war Britain still drab with rationing, shortages and an atmosphere of austerity. The bridegroom, who was created Duke of Edinburgh just before the wedding, was already popular in his wife's country; the son of Prince Andrew of Greece and Queen Victoria's granddaughter Princess Alice, he had been largely brought up in Britain by his uncle, Lord Louis Mountbatten (who in 1947, after presiding as Viceroy over Indian Independence, was created Earl Mountbatten of Burma). Fair, good-looking and forthright, the Prince had served in the Royal Navy during the war and been mentioned in despatches; off-duty he excelled at the favoured royal sports of polo, sailing and shooting. 'Everybody knows that the marriage of Elizabeth and Philip was a love-match – as that of Queen Victoria and the Prince Consort was', the historian A. L. Rowse wrote in *Vogue*. Unlike that of Queen Victoria, however, the future Queen Elizabeth's wedding took place 'surrounded by the full resources of press, radio, television and newsreels'. The first such ceremony to be broadcast live from Westminster Abbey, it heralded a new age of royal reporting.

The couple's first child, and future heir to the throne, Prince Charles, was born just over a year later, in November, 1948. In marking the event, *Vogue* published an article by the historian Arthur Bryant, which began entertainingly, 'A hundred and thirty years ago, it looked as if the monarchy was doomed.' During his own boyhood, he reflected, 'newspapers habitually attacked the Royal Family in the most insulting terms. Today . . . no newspaper with a popular circulation could maintain its sales if it did so.' The Crown had become both 'an essential part of the democratic machinery of government' and a symbol of its subjects' ideals, so that in times of crisis or 'national emotion', the British people now turned instinctively to the 'familiar, cherished family which occupies and surrounds the Throne'. It was, increasingly, as a family, rather than as stately figureheads, that Britain's royalty was now regarded. When the Princess Elizabeth's second child, Princess Anne, was born in 1950, Beaton's official portraits broke with tradition, showing the future Queen playing in the garden with her two-year-old, Prince Charles. And when, early in 1952, King George VI died in his sleep, aged only 56, his people mourned as for a personal loss. In its tribute to his unstinting service, and 'rigorous, unswerving, high ideals', *Vogue* wrote, 'His people loved him ... (as) both their King and their friend.'

Both at home and abroad, the Coronation of the new Queen Elizabeth II, on 2 June 1953, aroused intense interest and enthusiasm. *Time* magazine put the young Queen on its cover; American *Vogue* observed, 'She holds the affection and admiration of a world which watched her grow up', publishing a 14-page feature on 'the pageantry of the Coronation'. British *Vogue* began its coverage as early as April, with an account of the nation's preparations, and six pages of fashion advice, accompanied by detailed Eric drawings. ('The dress you will wear, if you are a peeress, will be long and slim, of white or cream-coloured material embroidered with gold or silver...') The official Coronation Issue included a portfolio of Beaton portraits of the chief participants in the great ritual – from the Archbishop of Canterbury and the Duke of Norfolk, to the Queen's Maids of Honour – and an article by Cecil Beaton, entitled 'Royal Album', in which he recalled his years as a royal photographer. A month later, *Vogue* carried his account of the ceremony itself, compiled from notes and sketches made during the service in Westminster Abbey. Beside his pen-and-ink drawings of pages and peeresses, the Queen with the Regalia, and the Prime Minister, Sir Winston Churchill, in his robes, Beaton wrote, 'This wonderful ceremony takes the mind back through a thousand years... This is history, but it is of today, living and new.' The novelist Elizabeth Bowen, watching the day's events from a crowd's-eye-view in the Mall, ended her report for American *Vogue* with a description of the Sovereign's returning procession: 'Eight home-going grey horses; four gold tritons. Seen through alternate windows of the coach is the head bowing the steadily-balanced crown ... we behold ELIZABETH, our undoubted Queen.'

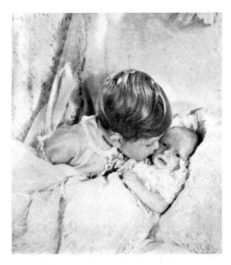

Above Prince Charles with Princess
Anne *Beaton*
Below At the Coronation: pages
and the Mistress of the Robes *Beaton*

Above Princess Margaret
and Antony Armstrong-Jones
Denis Manton
Opposite Queen Elizabeth II
Below Princess Anne and Captain Mark
Phillips *Parkinson*

In the rapidly-changing world of the 1950s and '60s, the Crown remained 'steadily balanced'. There was no diminution of State splendour, as *Vogue* photographs showed: visiting monarchs and presidents were still received with all the panoply of banquets and barouche-landaus, and the great royal ceremonies, such as the State Opening of Parliament, the Trooping the Colour on the Queen's official birthday, and the 600-year-old rites of the Order of the Garter, at Windsor, continued untouched by time. Yet the monarchy was skilfully modernised. Through television and public appearances, contact with ordinary people was increased; outdated customs were discarded; and in 1957 debutantes ceased to be presented at Court, thus ending the formal connection between royalty and an increasingly irrelevant 'social season'. 'The severance of this association in the post-war period by the Palace was perhaps its most brilliant decision', Sir Roy Strong wrote in 1979, in an article for *Vogue* on 'The Royal Image'.

Royalty's contemporary image was heightened, in the spring of 1960, by the marriage of the Queen's sister, Princess Margaret, with 'a hard-working, handsome photographer', Antony Armstrong-Jones. A frequent contributor to both American and British *Vogue*, the Earl of Snowdon, as he became, was one of the new generation of talented – and fashionable – young British photographers; as a member of the royal family he continued with his own career, working in the arts and the media. It was Lord Snowdon who, in 1969, supervised the arrangements for the Investiture of Prince Charles as Prince of Wales, at Caernarvon Castle. *Vogue* called it, 'The most original and direct ceremony ever devised to proclaim a prince', and the sight of the 21-year-old prince taking the oath of allegiance to his mother the Queen, amid the ancient splendour of Caernarvon, caught the imagination of the world.

Both the Prince of Wales and his sister, Princess Anne, had been given as normal an upbringing as possible – mixing with other children at boarding schools, and pursuing their own interests, as well as preparing for their future roles in public life. The royal love of horses had been inherited, in particular, by Princess Anne, whose 19th birthday photographs, by Norman Parkinson, showed her riding 'High Jinks' at Windsor; by the early 1970s, the Princess had emerged as a top-class horse-woman, and she was to represent Great Britain in the 1976

The Queen's Jubilee:
Bleached-out commemorative portrait
Snowdon

The Queen and the people
Joe Bulaitis

Olympic Games. It was through the world of equestrian sport that the Queen's only daughter met the man she was to marry: another Olympic competitor, Captain Mark Phillips.

Over the years *Vogue* had shown Princess Anne as a child in jodhpurs or bridesmaid's dresses, and as a '60s teenager, in pop prints and fashionably short skirts; later, in birthday portraits by Snowdon and Norman Parkinson, she had appeared as a thoughtful and beautiful young woman. But the 'Royal Wedding' issue of November, 1973, revealed a ravishing fairy-tale Princess, glittering in diamonds and furs, or posing in the Long Gallery at Windsor Castle in a floating white evening dress by Zandra Rhodes, her future husband beside her in scarlet mess kit. The photographs, by Norman Parkinson, established an indelible impression of Princess Anne, recalling the effect of Cecil Beaton's studies of Queen Elizabeth the Queen Mother, almost thirty-five years earlier. As Roy Strong later wrote, in his 'Royal Image' article, the Court painters of earlier eras had been replaced by photographers.

At the time of her Silver Jubilee, in 1977, the Queen's image was everywhere – on 'plastic bags, sweatshirts and hologram pendants', *Vogue* recorded, as well as on the more traditional mugs and biscuit-tins, such as had been designed for her predecessors. *Vogue*'s issue contained a special supplement, which compared the Queen's life and times, interests and travels, with those of former Queens of England; and a feature in December looked back on the year's events. There had been many similarities with the Jubilee of her grandfather, King George V, from the grand Naval Review to the special service of Thanksgiving at St Paul's – at which the Queen and Princess Margaret once again wore pink, as they had in 1935, as children. But the Queen had travelled further in twelve months than her predecessors did in a lifetime, from Western Samoa and Australia to Canada and the Bahamas; and the crowds who gathered outside Buckingham Palace to cheer her appearances with her family on the balcony numbered some 500,000 – greater even than on historic VE night. Much had changed; much, reassuringly, remained the same.

In February, 1981, *Vogue* published a group of new portraits by Snowdon which included two photographs of the youngest daughter of Earl Spencer. Within a month, it was announced that

Lady Diana Spencer and the Prince of Wales were engaged to be married. 'The camera has a unique capacity to conserve a moment of time', *Vogue* had written beside the Snowdon photographs; for a while, it seemed as if every moment in the future Princess's life were being conserved by the camera. She was everything the media could have dreamed of – pretty, interesting, photogenic; fond of children and tireless in her round of engagements; and she provided a brilliant new focus for British fashion. For her first evening appearance with the Prince, at a gala recital, she wore a dramatic evening dress by the Emanuels: not only was it decolleté, it was black – a colour previously reserved by royalty for mourning (though the Queen Mother had once posed, memorably, for Cecil Beaton in a black velvet dress by Norman Hartnell). Victorian Court mourning conventions had suddenly ceased to seem relevant, in 1981; and from then on younger members of the royal family were often seen in fashionable black and white. Throughout her engagement, every detail of Lady Diana's wardrobe was noted and copied, from her frilled collars and flat pumps to her distinctive, layered, blonde hair – 'one of the most charming short hairstyles we've seen in a long time', American *Vogue* enthused. For the first time since the beautiful Alexandra of Denmark married Queen Victoria's heir in 1863, and set a fashion for high collars of pearls, a British Princess had become a role-model for young women's style: in France, Italy, the United States, as well as in Britain. She even (as *Vogue* pointed out) led a revival in 'Princess of Wales' pearl chokers.

Lady Diana Spencer *Snowdon*

The wedding of the Prince of Wales and Lady Diana Spencer, on 29 July, 1981, was watched by millions, all over the world. *Vogue*'s report, in the September issue, captured details of crowds and carriages, of jewels and military uniforms; there was a charming pastel sketch by Feliks Topolski of the youngest bridesmaid, Winston Churchill's great-granddaughter Clementine Hambro, and photographs by Patrick Lichfield of the bridal party. The Princess of Wales's wedding-dress, by the Emanuels, was of ivory-coloured silk taffeta, with big puffed sleeves, slightly reminiscent of an Emanuel design which had appeared in *Vogue* in June. As the Archbishop of Canterbury said in his address during the ceremony, this day was the stuff of which fairy-tales were made.

Wedding Day *Bailey*

Norman Hartnell at work
Francis Marshall

At a fashion show:
the Queen Mother and Princess
Margaret with Lady Pamela
Berry and Hardy Amies

As the punk era of the '70s gave way to the '80s, marriage and motherhood, and more conservative values, came back into fashion. The Princess of Wales gave a lead, with her openly-expressed commitment to family life; she supported children's charities, such as Barnardo's and Birthright, involved herself with the work of marriage guidance, and set a precedent by taking her first child, Prince William (born in June, 1982), with her on a tour of Australia and New Zealand in 1983. In Sydney and Auckland, as in London and Cardiff, the Prince and Princess of Wales drew vast, enthusiastic crowds; and on subsequent tours throughout the world they met with similar receptions. In the 1980s, the international appeal of royalty seemed greater than ever.

Queen Victoria had warned her daughter-in-law Alexandra, as Princess of Wales, against 'too much dressing or smartness'; and for decades royal style tended to stand apart from fashion. (One notable exception, in the '30s, was Princess Marina – but her 'sense of fashion', American *Vogue* wrote, 'rather bothered . . . the British, who often prefer a discreet timelessness in the costume of their royalty'.) Queen Mary evolved a uniquely timeless mode of dress, with long sweeping skirts, buttoned shoes and, invariably, a toque. As *Vogue* photographs showed, it was a look which scarcely changed from the First World War until her death in 1953; yet on the day of her Jubilee, in 1935, the exacting John McMullin, of American *Vogue*, called her 'the most glamorous woman in the world', and wrote simply, 'I wondered how any one could have been better dressed.' A few years later, an article on Queen Elizabeth (now the Queen Mother), noted 'She follows her own taste and royal tradition rather than fashion', describing her preferences for simple feminine lines – 'which change little from season to season' – and 'soft flower colours' for day, with small hats which allowed the public to see her face clearly. 'But it is by night', the writer added, 'that queenliness comes into its own . . . (when) the jewelled, decolleté magnificence of royal dress sets a standard no ordinarily chic woman can hope to equal.'

After the war, the 'royal tradition' in dress became freer: Queen Elizabeth – dressed by Hardy Amies and, later, Ian Thomas, as well as Norman Hartnell – showed a preference for bright, distinctive colours and hats with touches of wit, such as the pink bells (by Frederick Fox) which she wore for her Jubilee.

But in the 1980s, the Princess of Wales brought a new spirit to royal – and British – fashion. She started popular trends for spotted socks and tasselled tights, for dinner-jackets worn by women and sparkly paste jewellery with bows; she wore chic, tailored coatdresses by Catherine Walker, suits by Rifat Ozbek and Arabella Pollen, luscious velvet, silk and satin ballgowns by Victor Edelstein, Bruce Oldfield, Murray Arbeid. For her 1988 visit to Paris she wore, as a special gesture, a red Chanel outfit; but in public the Princess of Wales was normally seen wearing clothes by British designers. Young, beautiful, and supremely well-dressed, she was giving royal patronage to fashion as an art, as an industry, and as a pleasure.

'The Royal Family's younger generation displays the same British dress sense that marks the most attractive of their contemporaries', the American novelist Joan Juliet Buck wrote in *Vogue* in September, 1986, reporting on the wedding of the Queen's second son, Prince Andrew, to Miss Sarah Ferguson. The occasion, she wrote, was 'spectacular ... and full of unexpected magic'. The bride, with flowers in her auburn hair, wore an ivory silk duchesse satin dress, by Lindka Cierach, with a train 17½ feet long; the Prince, who had served as a helicopter pilot in the Falklands war, was in naval uniform. That morning, he had been created Duke of York, the traditional title of the monarch's second son, and it was as the Duke and Duchess of York that the couple emerged from Westminster Abbey, watched by some half-billion people all around the world. 'Above all else', *Vogue* reported, 'The Duke and Duchess of York married in happiness.'

In the eighty-year span of Condé Nast's *Vogue*, the 'ceremonial side of life' had changed out of all recognition. And yet, looking through the past issues over eight decades, there is a constant sense of 'plus ça change' ... What a 1910 article on etiquette called 'the interest attaching to the royal life at Buckingham Palace' remains ever-potent; and after two World Wars, three Coronations, an Abdication, and two Silver Jubilees, Royalty is still in *Vogue*.

The Princess of Wales
with Bruce Oldfield
Rex Features

Manolo Blahnik's design
for the Duchess's wedding-shoe

FANFARE AND CEREMONY

... The coronation of a King of England is one production that is not to be derailed by any vagaries of cast, audience or fate. The office of King is, by its very nature, impregnable to death – or default. In the Chapel of the Garter in Westminster Abbey hang the banners of all the Knights of that most noble Order, over the shields with their armorial bearings; as each one dies, his banner is removed from above his place, to be supplanted by his successor's. Only one flag never comes down off the wall – the royal standard ...

And so – with a new leading man – the rehearsal for the Coronation goes on. The date of May 12, 1937, remained unchanged; England picked up her fevered preparations where she had left them off. Because a Queen will kneel at the altar beside the King, peeresses will bring coronets to the Abbey. That is the only difference: a sudden flash of gold at the moment of the crowning of the Queen, as peeresses raise the coronets and put them on their heads.

A world fed on distorted celluloid reproductions of its past, surfeited with synthetic splendour, will have the opportunity to look upon a pageant that is real, will see the kingly part played by a King, apparelled according to ancient tradition ... Here is no makeshift, but 'a kingdom for a stage, princes to act and monarchs to behold'.

Upon the twenty-seven-year-old Duke of Norfolk, Hereditary Marshal of England, Premier Duke and Premier Marshal, the cares of office weigh heavily. In issuing his orders for the robes to be worn by peers and peeresses, he declared 'that the robe or mantle of a baroness be of crimson velvet, the cape to be furred with miniver pure ... and the train to be three feet on the ground.' The quantities of each increase with rank until finally four rows of ermine, five inches of miniver, six feet of train distinguish a duchess from a mere baroness ...

Legend and ritual, gold and jewels from all over the world, down the ages, are woven into the fabric of the Coronation. No wonder that thousands are coming from the far corners of the earth to trim the streets, the windows and the rooftops when George VI and Queen Elizabeth take their serpentine route through London towards the 'great solempnytie' of their Coronation at the Abbey Church of St Peter's, Westminster.

From NOTES IN THE ABBEY 1953 Cecil Beaton

... At six o'clock the stream of arriving guests: dignitaries in cockaded hats, black velvet tam-o'-shanters, grey top hats... Guests from every world, and from every part of it...

The massed Peeresses, an inconceivably wonderful sight... Their foam-white ermine and dark red velvet looking like a parterre of auricula-eyed Sweet William... Their decolletage the palest pampered pink... Nothing in the world could be more elegant... Among them, undoubtedly the most beautiful is the young Duchess of Devonshire, wearing the original eighteenth-century coronation robes belonging to Georgiana, Gainsborough's Duchess, completely different in their cut and line...

Somehow the music of violin, trumpet and voice welling up through the tall grey vaults of the Abbey sounds more pure and sifted than it might anywhere else... The Processions begin... The golden carpet is the perfect floor covering for the slippered feet, for the scarlet uniform, the crimson robes of the Peers, the dark velvets of the Knights of the Garter, the white and gold copes of the Bishops... The general colour effect is of red, gold and smoke blue... Everywhere the motif of the Queen's crown...

This wonderful ceremony takes the mind back through a thousand years, yet it is as fresh and inspiring as some great histrionic ritual... The supreme nobility of the words of the service has the double impact of surprise and familiarity that greets the mark of real inspiration...

Always one's eye is beguiled by the unexpected effect... A mote of light catches a gold sequin fallen on the floor or a jewel in a Bishop's ring... The sun comes down and lights up the massed treasure of gold plate...

This is history, but it is of today, living and new... There is no pretence or make-believe about this great display... Perhaps in other countries such men as these might seem to be in fancy dress, but here they wear their gold thread embroideries with the insouciance born of total conviction...

The Queen has the suggestion of a smile which lightens the mouth... Her touching beauty at the Anointing, without her crown, like a child in a simple white dress... Then, her Byzantine magnificence in the stiff bell-shaped brocade that has come straight from the Ravenna mosaics...

THE STATE OPENING OF PARLIAMENT
'The King and Queen in the State Coach drawn by eight creamy horses on their way
to open Parliament': King George V and Queen Mary *top 1914* and *above 1935*
Right, Queen Elizabeth II opens Parliament *1958 B. Saidman*

TROOPING THE COLOUR
The Sovereign's Birthday Parade:
Above Queen Elizabeth II *1969 Camera Press*
Opposite King George VI flanked by his brothers,
the Duke of Gloucester and the Duke of Kent *1939*

CORONATION DAY
Coronation robes for a peer
and peeress *1953 Eric
Opposite* 'A sudden flash
of gold . . . as peeresses raise
the coronets and put them
on their heads'
1937 Horst

CORONATION CAVALCADE
Above Sir Winston Churchill, in the State robes
he wore at the Coronation *1953 Toni Frissell*
Below left and right Sir Winston Churchill
and the Duke of Edinburgh, drawn by Cecil Beaton
during the ceremony *1953*

Opposite Pages to the Duke
of Norfolk *1953 Parkinson*
Preceding pages: Left Maids of Honour
to the Queen *1953 Beaton*
Right The newly-crowned Queen
Elizabeth II *1953 Beaton*

Above King George VI *1937*
Opposite Queen Elizabeth II in Garter Robes – 'the plumed hat, the Sovereign's mantle
in dark sapphire velvet, and the collar of the Order' *1956 Beaton*

Above On the balcony at Buckingham Palace, celebrating the Silver Wedding
of King George VI and Queen Elizabeth: *l to r* Princess Elizabeth, the Duke
and Duchess of Gloucester, the King and Queen, Princess Margaret, Queen Mary *1948*

Opposite Celebrating the Silver Jubilee of Queen Elizabeth II,
l to r Prince Edward, Prince Andrew, Lord Mountbatten, the Queen, the Duke of Edinburgh,
Captain Mark Phillips, Princess Anne, Queen Elizabeth the Queen Mother
1977 Graphic Photo Union

ROYAL WEDDINGS

From THE WEDDING OF THE PRINCESS MARY 1922

It was fitting that pageantry should attend the marriage of the King's daughter, and that a wedding watched with so much love and loyalty should take place in the historic setting, with all its age-long beauty, of Westminster Abbey.

It was indeed the Fairy Princess, with Youth, Beauty and Happiness as her attendants, who drove, radiant in her glass coach, among her people – a delicate figure in white with small wreathed head, smiling her thanks to the great crowds thronging the streets to see her pass and shouting their good wishes and blessings to her. Later, through the great West door of the Abbey, she walked slowly up the long aisle in grave beauty, her hand in her father's, in a magical dress of shimmering white, cobwebbed with a myriad pearls and a train of spun silver and lace. Behind her the eight lovely bridesmaids in silver dresses streamed like bright ribbons from her train, their heads veiled, like the bride's, in misty tulle. Princess Maud and Lady Mary Cambridge held the wonderful length of train, and after them came those two dark beauties, Lady Mary Thynne and Lady Rachel Cavendish, followed by the smaller, but lovely pair, Lady Elizabeth Bowes-Lyon and Lady Doris Gordon-Lennox.

The sanctuary of the Abbey was full of sunlight falling in richly-coloured patterns on the gold and silver of the altar, on the gorgeous vestments of the Archbishops, on uniforms and gold lace, and on the array of fine dresses.

Three golden thrones were arranged within the altar rails for the King, the Queen and the Queen-Mother. Queen Mary, in royal and stately beauty, in her gown of wonderful gold lamé and parchment-coloured velvet, had the vivid blue of the Garter across the gold of her corsage, and the same bright note of colour appeared in the velvet on which her toque of gold tissue was mounted, the splendid panache of the white aigrette being just tipped with gold. Queen Alexandra was in soft orchid velvet, with a diadem-like toque of iridescent sequins, mauve, purple and blue.

But it seemed that, although the dresses of the exquisite figure of the bride, those of her silver maids and of the two Queens were the centre of interest in their loveliness, the magnificent attire of the guests was almost equal in splendour. No pains had been spared, and the wonderful stuffs, the colouring and designing formed an especial tribute to the great occasion.

From THE NEW YORKS 1986 Joan Juliet Buck

The charm of the wedding went beyond the pageantry. The delight came from the way Prince Andrew and Miss Ferguson remained themselves. What the various audiences (the hundreds in the Abbey, the thousands in the street and the millions viewing television) expected was pomp and solemn circumstance; they got that, but they also got winks, smiles and fingers pointed at them. For once, the Empire cheered back. Above everything else, the Duke and Duchess of York married in happiness...

Miss Ferguson's dress was the perfect union of formal shape and personal inclination. The fabric and bodice were eighteenth-century, and the skirt had a nineteenth-century bustle; the greatest moments of England were evoked. But the details, the embroidered bees, thistles and initials, were deeply personal to Miss Ferguson and Prince Andrew, the two individuals who ceased to exist during the marriage ceremony. And to honour this transformation, the personal emblems were marked out in delicate silver embroidery and woven into the net, so that the details would remain imperceptible for the television audience of half a billion people, but be striking for the more restricted audience in Buckingham Palace and the larger one in the Abbey.

The day of the wedding was cold; policemen admitted to shivering outside the gates of the Abbey. Many in the crowds had slept outside, although the day was not a holiday. Some had painted their faces with Union Jacks. The police had cleared the streets, and at 9-30 am they removed an amorous pair of stray dogs from the west door of the Abbey. The official recorders had been stacked like old letters in two wooden file boxes...

The play is written as a pageant. Yet while Miss Sarah Ferguson entered the Abbey with a crown of flowers and a certain nervous concentration in her father's eyes, the Duchess of York marched down the aisle more connected to the guests in the Abbey than when she had walked in: so aware of her friends, so happy at their presence, so open to the outside world, so utterly unselfconscious about her new status and its consequence and so full of communicable good spirits that the guests, the thousands in the streets and the half billion watching television were brought into her own private exultation...

ENGAGEMENTS
Top Princess Patricia of Connaught, granddaughter of Queen Victoria,
on her rumoured engagement to a German prince *1913 Underwood and Underwood*
Above left Princess Alexandra, Duchess of Fife, great-granddaughter
of Queen Victoria *1913 Speaight*
Above right Her fiancé Prince Arthur of Connaught,
brother of Princess Patricia *1913 W & D Downey*
Opposite Lady Elizabeth Bowes-Lyon on her engagement to the future
King George VI *1923 Maurice Beck and Macgregor*

CLASSICAL BRIDES
Above Princess Marina of Greece, engaged to the Duke of Kent *1934 Horst*
Opposite Lady Alice Montagu-Douglas-Scott, engaged to the Duke of Gloucester *1935 Beaton*

Above Princess Margaret, a portrait by her future husband Antony Armstrong-Jones *1960*
Opposite Princess Alexandra, daughter of the Duke and Duchess of Kent,
with her future husband the Hon Angus Ogilvy *1963 Beaton*

Above The Prince of Wales, on his engagement
to Lady Diana Spencer *1981 Snowdon*
Opposite Princess Anne with her fiancé Captain Mark Phillips,
in the Long Gallery at Windsor Castle *1973 Parkinson*

Future Princesses Royal, on their engagements:
Above Princess Mary, only daughter of King George V
(created Princess Royal 1932) *1922 Alice Hughes*
Opposite Princess Anne, only daughter of Queen Elizabeth II
(created Princess Royal 1987) *1973 Parkinson*

WEDDING DAYS
Above Prince and Princess Arthur of Connaught and their attendants;
Princess Mary is the bridesmaid back left *1913 Alexander Corbett*
Opposite The Princess of Wales's youngest bridesmaid, Clementine Hambro,
great-granddaughter of Sir Winston Churchill *1981 Feliks Topolski*
Preceding pages: Left The Princess of Wales *1981 Lichfield*
Right The Duchess of York *1986 Rex Features*

Above Queen Alexandra and
Queen Mary leaving the wedding
of Lord and Lady Louis
Mountbatten *1923*
Left and right King George V and
Queen Mary with the Kaiser
and Kaiserin, at a family
wedding in Berlin *1913*
Below Lady Elizabeth Bowes-
Lyon before her wedding *1923*

Princess Mary and her bridegroom, Viscount Lascelles *1922 C Vandyk*

Princess Mary's wedding dress, by Reville 'The underdress was of silver lamé, over which was a slip of marquisette embroidered with pearls and crystal beads in a trelliswork of roses . . . The lovely train was of ivory duchess satin woven with silver in a design of emblematic flowers. Round the edge of the train were lotus flowers which were embroidered in India, and the Honiton lace bordering it was worn by the Queen' *1922*

Princess Marina's wedding dress, by Molyneux – 'supple lamé with a raised flower design in silver; clouds of tulle held by a tiara; a draped neck, graceful sleeves, a princesse line, a great Court train of the same lamé; and the sum total is that simple perfection of chic which distinguishes her whole Molyneux trousseau' *1934*

Above Princess Elizabeth and her husband, the Duke of Edinburgh,
leading their wedding in the Glass Coach *1947 Graphic Photo Union*
Opposite Princess Elizabeth entering Westminster Abbey on the arm
of her father, King George VI. Her dress, by Hartnell, was 'starred,
with Botticelli-like delicacy and richness, with pearl and crystal
roses, wheat, orange blossom' *1947 Pix*

Above Princess Margaret and her husband, in their going-away car *1960*
Opposite Princess Margaret and Antony Armstrong-Jones leaving their wedding *1960 Duffy*
Overleaf The Prince and Princess of Wales after their wedding in St Paul's Cathedral *1981 Freson*

NEWLY MARRIED
Above Lord and Lady Louis Mountbatten *1923 Danford Barney*
Opposite Prince and Princess Michael of Kent *1978 Parkinson*

FAMILY LIFE

From EDUCATION OF A PRINCESS 1937

... The heir-presumptive to the throne of England, the Empire of India and the monarchy of all the British Dominions beyond the seas is today a princess and not a prince, and whatever may be said about the curious proposition, the equality of the sexes, it is obvious that the education of a prince to be a king is a far different thing from the education of a princess to be a queen.

Then there is the undoubted fact that the education of anybody at all has become a highly intricate affair: the last time the problem of educating a queen confronted a royal parent it was uncomplicated by the modernist methods of Montessori and the dire warnings of Freud that now haunt the parent and rule the preceptor. One thing is recognised that has never been acknowledged before in the schooling of an English queen – that whatever state awaits her she has a right to be happy as a child...

Queen Elizabeth, it is well known, holds very definite views about her children's upbringing...

In one thing Princess Elizabeth's life is very unlike that of her great-great-grandmother Victoria. When a child Princess Victoria never had a room of her own; until she came to the throne she slept in her mother's bedroom and had no place where she might sit or work by herself. Princess Elizabeth has a pleasant sitting-room in the five-room suite at Buckingham Palace that has been prepared for the royal children. In this, her first kingdom, a sixteen-by-twenty space, devoted to lessons, meditations and the general conduct of life, the Princess takes great delight. It is equipped with an electric heater and an impressive work desk, lighted with most modern efficiency. Here England's heir already maintains her privacy, and even those favoured people, her aunts and uncles, must knock and await an invitation to enter. Her sister, Princess Margaret Rose, still in the nursery stage, does not take lessons with her...

Among diversions that the sisters share, cooking has an interesting place. They have their own stove in their miniature house and produce some wonderful messes. Gardening is another thing they love, they both have the modern craze for bicycling, and both have regular swimming lessons at the Bath Club. Princess Elizabeth has also acquired very early the royal taste for photography...

From THE DUKE AND DUCHESS OF KENT AT HOME 1938

... The Duke and Duchess of Kent, with or without an audience, retain their private simplicity. They have, as Dr Johnson might say, 'elevated good taste to a Public Duty' ...

Good taste has always been a public duty with the Duchess. One of three princesses, part Russian, part Danish, the daughters of Prince Nicolas and Princess Helene of Greece, she was born in Athens in a villa given as a wedding present to her parents by the Czar. In the last days of the splendour of the Czar's court, she journeyed to St Petersburg and the palace of her grandmother, the Grand Duchess Vladimir. Later, war and revolution drove her family from country to country ... Recalled triumphantly to Athens, they were shut out again, and this time, in the brilliant 'Twenties, exiled to Paris. There, far from the *operette* unreality of pre-War royalty, Princess Marina was brought up ...

At their town house in Belgrave Square, the Duke possesses a superb miniature library with pictures and objets, carefully chosen by himself. There, he has his collection of jades, of watches, his piano and his gardens. The lilies which he grows, the Duchess arranges. In fact, all the flowers at 'Coppins', their country place, are arranged by the Duchess, who also does the window-boxes at Belgrave Square. Much of her time goes into sketching and painting (portraits rather than landscapes); into reading, particularly memoirs; into entertaining, for her reputation as a hostess is as great as her reputation for chic. Most of their weekends, of course, are spent at 'Coppins', and the life there, of knitting and gardening, looks like a Dutch interior of domestic happiness.

At weekends throughout the summer, the Duke and Duchess of Kent head for the country, like the rest of us. No stately home for them, with freedom cramped by formality and the hard work of large house parties ... Two spare rooms limit the guests. Servants are few, nurses not in evidence, as the children play with their parents and ride the pony. Their father plays the piano and tends the garden. The mother (with her hair brushed up in the current manner) sketches, knits, embroiders. A royal family enjoys being simply a family.

Above The former Princess Patricia of Connaught with her son, Alexander *1920 Central News Service*
Opposite The Duke and Duchess of York with their first daughter, Princess Elizabeth *1926 Marcus Adams*

Princess Elizabeth with her mother, the Duchess of York
1927 Marcus Adams

Princess Elizabeth with her grandmother, Queen Mary
1927 Marcus Adams

Above Princess Mary, Viscountess Lascelles, with her sons
George, left (the present Earl of Harewood), and Gerald *1926 Speaight*
Opposite The former Princess Patricia at Clarence House
with her husband, the Hon Alexander Ramsay, and their son
Alexander. Her father, the Duke of Connaught, left, was the son
of Queen Victoria, godson to the Duke of Wellington,
victor of Waterloo, and godfather of the present Queen Elizabeth II
1923 Pacific and Atlantic

Above left Princess Elizabeth aged two *1929 Marcus Adams*
Above right With her mother the Duchess of York *1930 Marcus Adams*
Below In party frills *1937 Marcus Adams*
Opposite Queen Elizabeth with the Princesses Elizabeth
and Margaret Rose at her family seat, Glamis Castle *1937 Central Press Photos*
Overleaf King George VI with the Princesses *1944 Studio Lisa*

Above Princess Alexandra with the Hon Angus Ogilvy and children Marina and James *1967 Beaton*
Opposite The Duke and Duchess of Kent, with Princess Alexandra and Prince Edward,
the present Duke *1941 Beaton*

GROWING UP
Above Prince Richard of Gloucester, the present Duke
of Gloucester, aged 9 *1953 Beaton*
Opposite Lady Helen Windsor, daughter of the present Duke
and Duchess of Kent, aged 11 *1975 Parkinson*

Above Princess Anne with her son Peter Phillips,
the Queen's first grandchild *1978 Snowdon*
Opposite The Princess of Wales with her second son,
Prince Harry *1984 Snowdon*

Above Queen Elizabeth at Windsor Castle with Princess Elizabeth
and Princess Margaret *1944 Beaton*
Opposite Princess Elizabeth at Buckingham Palace with her first child,
Prince Charles *1948 Beaton*

Above The Queen with Princess Anne, dressed for their favourite sport *1959 Parkinson*
Opposite The Duke of Edinburgh with his grandchildren,
Princess Anne's son and daughter Peter and Zara Phillips *1984 Tim Graham*
Preceding pages: Left Prince William of Gloucester, elder son
of the Duke and Duchess of Gloucester *1944 Lee Miller*
Right Prince William of Wales, elder son of the Prince and Princess
of Wales *1984 Tim Graham*

THE WINDSOR STORY

From JOTTED DOWN BY WALLIS WINDSOR 1943

Like everybody else, we live from hand to mouth, for flexibility is a great wartime necessity... Government House is on a completely wartime schedule... The Duke spends all day at his office; I spend mine at the United Services Canteen, the Negro Canteen, the Red Cross, and the two Infant Welfare Clinics that we founded... I must be at the Canteen some time every day, and I often go into the kitchen to lend a hand...

The secret of running an attractive house is the personal touch... I enjoy housekeeping... In wartime, I have to make just whirlwind tours every morning and see that all is in order...

In wartime especially, my clothes philosophy on the Island, as everywhere, is simply to look neat, appropriate, and inconspicuous... (Never the sensational dress.)... I don't give much time to clothes, as mine are just correct, well-cut and of good materials, allowing me to wear them for several years... Since I can't be pretty, I try to look sophisticated, but, unfortunately, I always want to be dressed like everybody else... When I am out I always feel dowdy, and wish that I had thought of getting that dress, and wearing it that way...

What you learn in your childhood about clothes stays with you all your life. I was rather poor and had to buy clothes that would do for the morning, for shopping, for the afternoon – practical, long-wearing, all-day dresses. I still buy that way...

The training of being poor is the most valuable one in the world – even if being poor doesn't last...

... Food rationing is stringent in Nassau and grumbling about war's adjustments, about any kind of war rationing, infuriates me... I never diet, but I do keep my weight around 112 by just being careful... For our constant dinners for military men we depend on chicken, Nassau's famous turtle pie, fish mousse and fruits, especially pineapple... For dessert we have perhaps papaya ice-cream, or a macedoine of fruits, and always a tray of American cheeses...

I have never really lived in a house that was my own, in the background I wanted...

From THE DUKE AND DUCHESS OF WINDSOR 1964 Valentine Lawford

The Duke visits England more often than his wife. She encourages him to do so, knowing that he enjoys seeing his lawyers and bankers and old friends and regimental comrades – even if it must be an eerie experience for him, of all Englishmen of the century, to walk down Piccadilly or St James's Street to all appearances unrecognized except by some elderly clubman with a Guards tie, nostalgically raising a respectful bowler hat. If he wishes her to go with him to England, she does so – most often before Christmas, modern Parisians having a weakness for presents bought in London. But England for her is too full of memories, some too bitter and all too poignant, for her to feel at peace, or entirely welcome there, even now.

Curiously, though, it is the Duchess who by this time more often uses an English word or phrase in place of its American equivalent...

Through some similar process, it is now the Duchess who has the more 'Royal' memory for names, and will know better than the Duke to which of his relatives this or that object once belonged, or whether some piece of furniture was already among his possessions at St James's Palace or Fort Belvedere. 'Oh, did that come with *me?*' is likely to be his only comment. In return, it is the former King who rather enjoys reminding his wife, the former commoner, that nowadays one must make more effort to move with the times.

In countless ways, mostly too slight to mention, their characters are mutually complementary. The Duke, for instance, is a man who loses things, and the Duchess is a woman who finds them. Perhaps inevitably one knows, or guesses, more of the strength she affords her husband than of any strength she may draw from him in return. Anyone who has been their guest will have sensed that the Duchess, even as she is at her most hospitable and entertaining, is always intensely concerned to assure herself that the Duke is not left out or feeling bored. But his own devotion is also proverbial.

Perhaps, too, the Duchess has found strength in the very difficulty of her role – in the enigma, which she admits, that her husband's Royalty still represents for her, in the curious abyss which it creates between him and all other men... How many other women, one wonders, could have filled the void where a Kingdom was...?

'English interest naturally centres now on the Prince of Wales...'
The future King Edward VIII, and Duke of Windsor, aged 19 *1913 Campbell Gray*

Top left and right The Prince of Wales in Canada 1919
Above left At the Derby *1923*
Above right Taking a fence on 'Little Favourite' *1923*

Above Edward VIII, King and Emperor *1936 Hugh Cecil*
Opposite 'The woman he loved', Wallis Warfield Simpson *1937 Beaton*

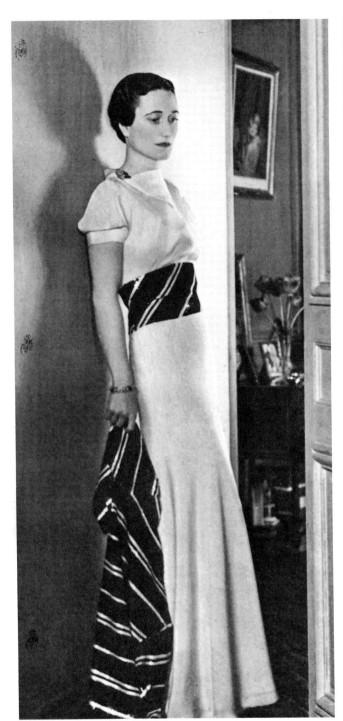

Above left Mrs Simpson, shortly before her wedding,
in a Mainbocher dress from her trousseau *1937 Beaton*
Above right The Duchess of Windsor, again wearing Mainbocher *1943 Beaton*
Opposite The Duke and Duchess of Windsor on their wedding-day,
at the Château de Candé *1937 Beaton*

Above The Duke and Duchess of Windsor in their first house, La Cröe, in Antibes *1938*
Below The Surrealist 'W'-shaped terrace table *1938*

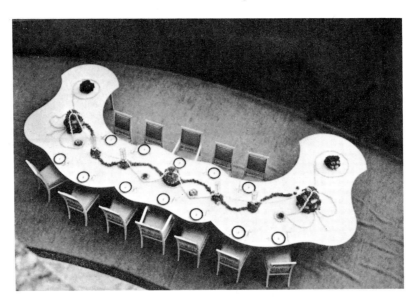

Above The Duke and Duchess in wartime, as Governor
and Governor's Lady of the Bahamas *1940*
Below left The Duchess, in Red Cross uniform, oversees
building work at Government House *1941 Rawlings*
Below right The Duke addresses
the Bahamas Labour Union *1941 Rawlings*

Above The Duchess of Windsor, wearing Dior *1949 Arik Nepo*
Opposite In her suite at the Hotel Meurice, the Duchess
photographed exclusively for *Vogue 1937 Horst*

THE WINDSORS' WORLD
Above left The Duchess shopping in Paris with her bodyguard *1937 Schall*
Above right At a benefit performance in New York
with Mr and Mrs Herman Rogers and her bodyguard *1941 Carswell*
Below left The Duke dancing with Mrs Henry Ford II *1951 Doisneau*
Below right The Duke and Duchess at a ball *1953 Boucher*
Overleaf: The Duke in favourite checks *left 1967 Lichfield*
Right 1964 Horst

The Duchess, wearing 'a meticulous grey suit' by Schiaparelli *1951 Beaton*

Above The Duke and Duchess at The Mill, their country house near Paris *1967 Lichfield*
Opposite The Duke's Bahamian valet, in evening livery, with the pugs *1964 Horst*
Preceding pages: Left Mrs Simpson *1937 Beaton*
Right The Duchess of Windsor, with Cartier lorgnette *1955 Bouché*

IN WAR AND PEACE

From PORTRAIT OF A QUEEN 1941 Audrey Stanley of Alderley

... Queen Elizabeth, small, dark, with pink and white complexion, deep-set eyes, strongly-marked eyebrows, wide mouth, soft voice and deep laugh, has captured everybody's heart. She is composed, considerate, and completely natural and unfailingly interested in everything she does...

It was characteristic of her to send for André Maurois to tell him how distressed she was for Paris and for the French people in their misfortune. The same night she broadcast to France, speaking with great emotion that came straight from the heart. Perhaps she felt that André Maurois could express with his pen what she had expressed with her voice. Later she visited wounded Free French soldiers – spoke to each one in turn. They all said when she left that she had given them new hope and courage.

... Both the King and Queen have always liked living simply, so they easily adopted a wartime regime. They are rationed like everyone else, and have plain meals. For dinner they have soup, then fish or game, and a sweet or savoury. Never more than three courses, sometimes only two...

The King and Queen have made many journeys to visit the people in badly bombed districts, and have seen sad sights with sorrow in their hearts, and mingled expressions of sympathy and indignation.

They travel either in a shrapnel-proof car or in the Royal Train which slows up but never stops during raids. The Royal coach serves as a palace on wheels, in which they sleep and have their meals...

Everywhere people have wanted to know whether the Queen has lost any of her belongings when Buckingham Palace was bombed – and to exchange sympathies with her. It was in fact her private sitting-room which suffered most and several of her favourite things were shattered.

When their Majesties arrived in Sheffield, the crowd cheered them gallantly and then broke down with emotion. A moving ceremony took place in a factory when at the request of the workpeople the managing director was knighted in their presence, instead of at Buckingham Palace. Then the King and Queen drove round the poorest and most badly hit part of the city. One of the crowd said to her neighbours: 'We couldn't have stood it if their Majesties had not come and showed us that they cared'.

From THE MOUNTBATTENS IN WARTIME 1943 Lesley Blanch

... Lord Louis' naval career was the undeviating trajectory-course of his life. An Osborne cadet in 1913, he saw active service in Beatty's fleet. After the war he specialised in signals, and perfected the Mountbatten Shutter, a special signalling device. Two years before the war he was responsible for the Mountbatten Station-Keeper, which is now installed in all the newest destroyers. He prefers the seamanship and personal qualities involved in handling destroyers, to the more static immensity of the bigger ships. He loves a seagoing life... He is an arrogant, vain, impulsive and dashing Captain, who, had he not such magnificent seamanship, might be dubbed slap-dash by the diehards. His men adore him...

No need to recall here the the many anecdotes of his furious fighting record, commanding the Kelly; in action off Norway; bringing the torpedoed Javelin back to port; swimming for his life, when the Kelly was finally sunk, off Crete; commanding the aircraft carrier, Illustrious, and then, in succession to Sir Roger Keyes, becoming 'Commando in Chief'. No need, here, to enlarge on his tactical skill, his enterprise and meticulous, split-second timing of all operations. His every move is history, now...

And Lady Louis? She too has met the challenge of reality with purpose and individuality. 'Just the wife of a Commando' is how she described herself, in a recent speech. Actually, she is something more. She is, in fact, Superintendent in Chief of the Joint Red Cross and St John Organisation... Her day begins at 7 am and often goes on till late in the evening. She tours the country organising and supervising, seeing for herself. She will not delegate... In 1941 she went to America on a tour for her St John Organisation, making speeches in all the seventeen cities she visited in twenty-one days.

During the worst of the blitz she worked in the shelters – the real ones – the fetid, lousy, damp, overcrowded shelters of the East End. She was there night after night, nursing, organising, improving. No polite bandaging for her... She is as avid for work as she used to be for play. She has had experience of hospital staff work too, working in the theatres... She is still, on the face of it, too shimmering, too elegant a creature to make her work in the operating theatres appear credible...

115

WARTIME SERVICE
Above Princess Mary with her brothers,
l to r, The Duke of York, the Duke of Kent
and the Duke of Gloucester
1918 Central News Service
Below left The Duchess of Kent,
'head of navy women' *1941 Beaton*
Below right King George VI and Queen Elizabeth,
inspecting bomb damage *1942 Beaton*

Lord Louis Mountbatten, Supreme Allied Commander,
South East Asia, at Broadlands with his family:
Edwina Mountbatten, in the uniform of the Joint
Red Cross and St John Organisation, and their daughters
Patricia, a WRNS rating, and Pamela, a Girl Guide
1943 Beaton

Above Princess Elizabeth, aged sixteen, as honorary
Colonel of the Grenadier Guards; her cap bears
the regimental insignia *1943 Beaton*
Opposite King George VI and Queen Elizabeth amongst
the bomb damage at Buckingham Palace *1945 Beaton*

THE NAVAL TRADITION
Above The Duke of York *1923 C Vandyk*
Opposite The Duke of Kent *1927 Maurice Beck and Macgregor*

SOLDIERS OF THE QUEEN
Above Princess Elizabeth inspecting troops in Kenya *1952 Keystone Pictures Inc*
Opposite The Queen about to present new colours to the Grenadier Guards at Buckingham Palace *1953 Parkinson*

Princess Elizabeth inspects the Grenadier Guards *1947 Eric*

Above The Prince and Princess of Wales with Prince Andrew and Prince Edward,
at the unveiling of a statue to Lord Mountbatten *1984*
Below The Queen Mother in Germany with the Irish Guards, wearing St Patrick's Day shamrocks
1984 Tim Graham
Overleaf Prince Andrew, with the Queen and the Duke of Edinburgh,
on his return from the Falklands *1982 Bryn Collon*

PEACETIME SERVICE
Above Princess Mary inspects the Boys' Brigade
1921 Kadel & Herbert News Service
Below Queen Mary inspects nurses *1939*

Princess Alice, Countess of Athlone, President of the National
Children Adoption Association, with one of the children *1924 Ionides*

Above left The Princess of Wales visiting a Barnardo's Home in Belfast *1986 Pacemaker Press*
Above right Prince Edward on a Duke of Edinburgh's Award Scheme
expedition *1986 Tim Graham*
Below Princess Anne, President of the Save the Children Fund,
in The Gambia *1984 Tim Graham*

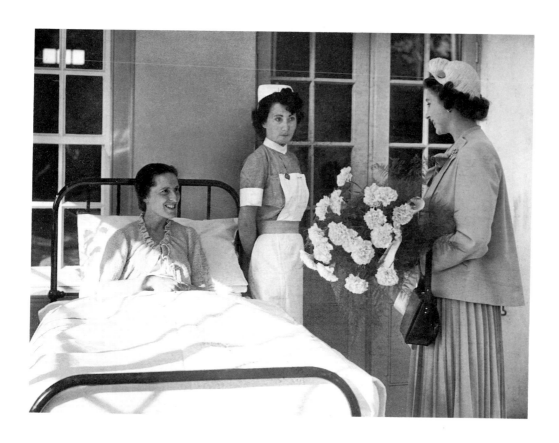

Above Princess Elizabeth visiting a Guernsey hospital *1949 Topical Press*
Below Princess Anne with nursing cadets *1981 Desmond O'Neill*

ABROAD AND AT HOME

From SCOTTISH SEASON 1937

... King George VI is a keen and efficient shot, loves his wife's country as much as she does, and has for many years run the sporting side of life at Balmoral with quiet efficiency... Shooting lunch parties organised by His Majesty combine simplicity with real comfort... Stalkers, of course, have to carry their lunches on their backs, so for them hot food is out of the question, but Queen Elizabeth herself supervises the packing of the knapsacks full of scones and cold meat, and sees to it that all the flasks are well filled.

King George likes nothing better than to return to his family circle after a long day on the hill, to have a real Scotch high tea (shortbread, heather honey, perhaps a poached egg) after a boiling bath, and then to read aloud to them until bedtime...

The new King and Queen, though perhaps slightly more inclined to formality than King Edward, both love young people, and both have a passion for dancing, so they will probably decide to revive the ghillies' dances for which Balmoral was famous in the old days. These ghillies' balls, supposedly given for the stalkers, gamekeepers and servants on the estate, used to be attended by many of the local 'Lairds' and their ladies as well, and a very gay picture they made, with the kilts and tartan scarfs flying as the dancers whirled in a reel or a country dance, played by the best pipers in the countryside. (King George's pipers were famous, and carried everything before them at the annual Braemar Gathering.)...

The Braemar Gathering is a unique event... Two years ago it was decided to abolish the march past of the Clansmen, a pity, many people thought, for they made a brave show, led by their pipers, with tartans and weapons gleaming in the sunshine. (The Braemar Gathering is generally lucky and enjoys real Royal weather.) There are rumours that the march past may be revived this year at the request of Queen Elizabeth, who is anxious that as many of the old Scotch traditions as possible should survive. In any case, the dancing and the pipe competitions are attractive enough to draw huge crowds every season. The Gathering, which takes place during the first week in September, is always attended by the King and Queen and a large party from Balmoral...

From HURRY, KING AND QUEEN! 1939 Stephen Leacock

All over Canada we are awaiting with great expectancy the visit of the King and Queen. I don't know yet what I shall wear – probably just a plain fedora hat over that linen suit I bought last year; or I may wait till I see first what the King does.

I'm not saying this in any personal sense, but merely to indicate that in Canada we are not thinking so much of what we shall wear, but of all the things that we want to show to the King and Queen...

It's the same, I say, all over Canada. It has nothing to do with forms and ceremonies, dignities and pretences – just the case of things that we feel we want them to see and not miss. Up in my home town on Lake Simcoe (My! I do hope the Queen can see Lake Simcoe on a June morning), up in my home town we feel it's such a shame that their visit will be just too early for the Lake Simcoe Herring Fishing – unless we can get them to stay over. In the Niagara peninsula they're afraid that the King and Queen will be just too late to see the peach trees in blossom; and up at Moose Factory, on the James Bay, they're afraid the ice will be gone before they come; indeed there's a rumour at Moose Factory that the King and Queen may not get there at all: which would be just a heart-break...

The truth is that all over the Empire has passed a wave of realisation of our common need each for all, our common danger and our only common salvation. This world isn't milk and water, this is 'guns and butter'; this isn't freedom, this is struggle. All men are brothers, but we're not going to be brothers first.

In which sense of common danger we turn everywhere to the Monarchy. Thank God that holds... We need the symbol for which these two gallant people stand, the continuity of our Monarchy, the link that has replaced the others, rusted out or filed away or carelessly broken asunder...

... Hurry, King and Queen! Hurry! We are all waiting. From the apple orchards of Annapolis, from the New Brunswick gardens of the valley of St John, heavy with drooping peonies, to where in the far-away Arctic delta of the Mackenzie the willow bushes awake to life and murmur of your coming... Hurry, King and Queen. We need you.

DUTIES AND DIVERSIONS
Above The Princess Royal, eldest daughter of Edward VII,
with a small flower-seller at a fête *1923*
Below Queen Elizabeth II tends a baby *1952 Graphic Photo Union*
Opposite On meeting Queen Mary *1953 Agence Intercontinentale*

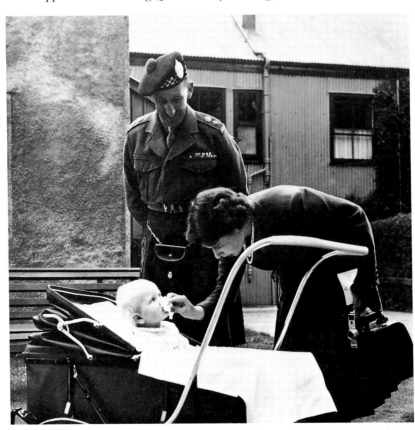

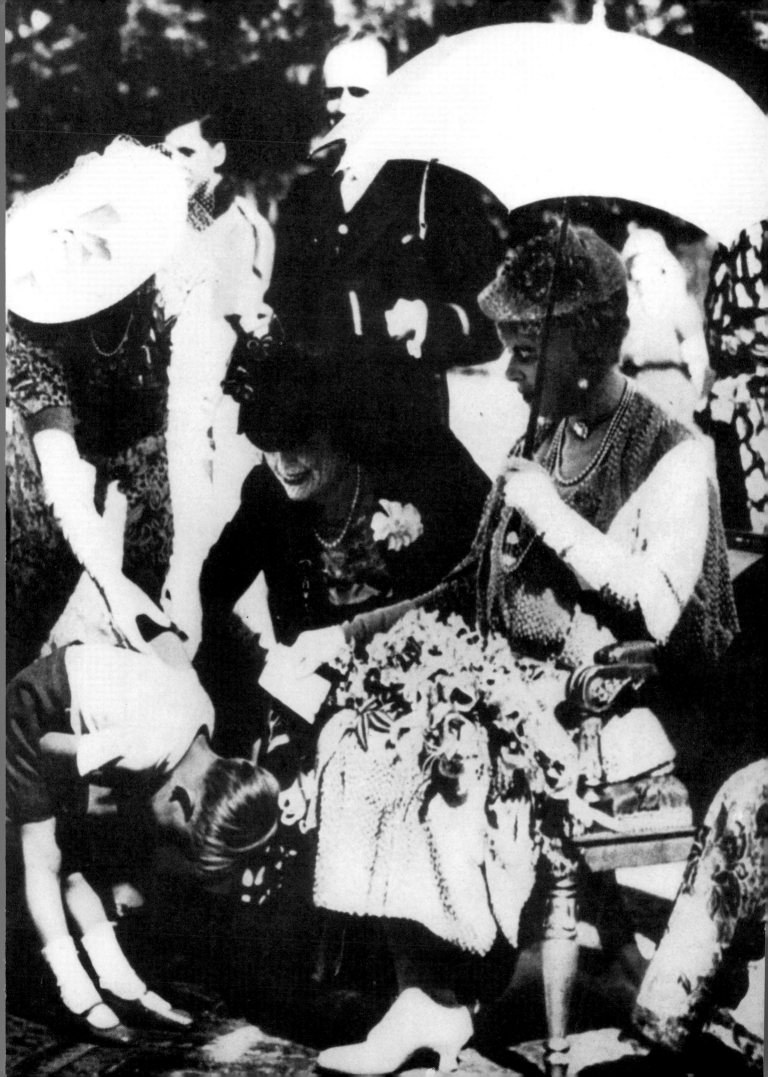

OUTDOOR APPEARANCES
Above left Queen Alexandra at the Chelsea Flower Show *1913*
Above right King George VI and Queen Elizabeth, with the Princesses,
at the annual Braemar Gathering, in Scotland *1939*
Below The future Princess of Wales, planting a tree in memory of Lord
Mountbatten at Broadlands, his Hampshire home *1981 Swaebe*

ROYALTY AND THE STAGE
Above left Princess Margaret with Sir Frederick Ashton at the Royal Opera House *1985 Desmond O'Neill*
Above right The Duchess of Kent meeting Renato Bruson, as Falstaff *1982 Desmond O'Neill*
Below The Queen Mother with Noel Coward *1968 Swaebe*

ROYAL TOURS
Above Renewing the Entente Cordiale, King George VI and Queen Elizabeth
on their pre-war visit to France, at the Elysée Palace
with President and Mme Lebrun *1938 Topical Press*
Opposite The King and Queen depart for their tour *1938*

Above Princess Elizabeth and the Duke of Edinburgh leaving for a tour of Kenya *1952*
Opposite King George VI and Queen Elizabeth watching their departure, at London Airport; Sir Winston
Churchill can be seen below. The King was to die shortly after, and the Princess returned to England as Queen
1952 Keystone

IN THE USA
Above Prince Philip and Lord Mountbatten, at a charity banquet in New York *1966*
Below President and Mrs Reagan with the Prince and Princess
of Wales at The White House *1986 Tim Graham*

IN BRITAIN
Above left The Queen at Windsor with the Amir of Bahrain *1984 Desmond O'Neill*
Above right With Mrs Reagan *1984 Rex Features*
Below The British Royal Family with the Danish Royal Family,
at a banquet at Claridges *1974 Press Association*

Above The Queen in Nepal *1986 Tim Graham*
Below Travelling by Royal Train *1984 Tim Graham*
Opposite The Princess of Wales
at the Sydney Opera House *1983 Lionel Cherrault*

Above The Prince and Princess of Wales, with Prince William
and Prince Harry, during their visit to Italy *1985 Tim Graham*
Below The Queen Mother in Venice *1985 Tim Graham*
Opposite The Princess of Wales in Florence *1985 Tim Graham*
Preceding pages: left Prince Charles and Lord Mountbatten in Kathmandu *1975 Sarah Bennett*
Right The Queen with Mrs Gandhi *1984 Tim Graham*

Above The Queen and the Duke of Edinburgh dancing
at a Ghillies' Ball at Balmoral *1953 Lichfield*
Opposite The Prince and Princess of Wales in New Zealand *1983 Lionel Cherrault*

Above Lady Elizabeth Bowes-Lyon, now Queen Elizabeth the Queen Mother, as a Spanish lady *1923*
Below left Lady Sarah Armstrong-Jones and Lady Helen Windsor,
dressed for a Raj party *1985 Camera Press*
Below right The Princess of Wales in Gold Rush costume, in Canada *1983 Tim Graham*

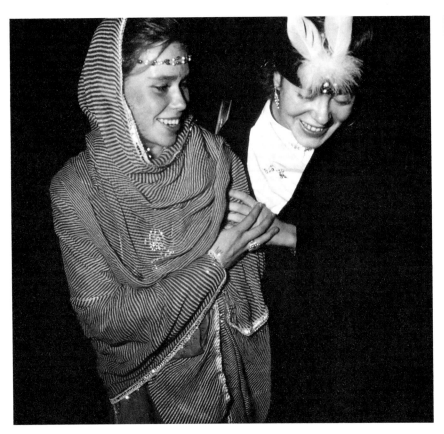

The Duchess of Kent, born Princess Marina of Greece, in national costume *1938 Beaton*

ROYAL SPORTS
Above The Royal Yacht Britannia,
at Cowes *1923*
Right Lady Elizabeth Bowes-Lyon,
ready for tennis *1922*
Below The Duke of Gloucester
with a shooting-party *1928*
and left At Henley *1923*

Above left King George V and his daughter Princess Mary riding in the Row *1913*
Above right The Duke of York hunting with the Pytchley *1928*
Below Princess Alexandra with her riding instructor *1946*
Overleaf King George V and Queen Mary at Ascot *1935*

SPORTS OF PRINCES
Playing polo: *Left* The Duke of
Gloucester *1924*
Right The Duke of Edinburgh
1957
Below The Prince of Wales *1984*
Opposite The Duke of Edinburgh
at the National Carriage Driving
Championships *1978*

Above Princess Elizabeth learning to ride *1930 Philip Mishon*
Opposite Princess Anne riding High Jinks at Windsor *1969 Parkinson*

ROYAL STYLE

From DRESS SENSE OF A QUEEN 1939

Queen Elizabeth is not a 'fashionable' woman in the usual sense of the world. Yet her clothes superbly fulfil the two fundamentals of good dressing. They fit her personality; and they are brilliantly suited to her way of life.

She feels that it is a Queen's place to follow, not fashion, but the grand tradition of royal dressing. The English people regard the throne as something enduring and constant in their lives. They do not want to see a different Queen each season – now Renaissance, now Directoire, now Victorian. They love the Queen they know, and they want her to stay that way. Queen Mary's clothes ten or fifteen years ago were almost identical with her clothes today. Queen Elizabeth is wise to follow her example, and choose lines which change little from season to season.

By day, she wears always a straight loose coat, either short, hip-length or finger-tip length, over a very simple matching dress. She has many long, full, lace garden-party dresses with loose matching jackets . . .

But it is by night that Queenliness comes into its own. By night the jewelled, decolleté magnificence of royal dress sets a standard no ordinarily chic woman can hope to equal. Last summer the splendour of Queen Elizabeth's gala dresses made them suddenly not only royal news, but front-page fashion news – when, following in the footsteps of the illustrious Empress Eugénie, she launched the second crinoline fashion in all its billowing glory. With these dresses she wears her magnificent jewellery . . .

Beside the two main tenets that influence the Queen's fashions – her personal taste and the royal tradition – certain technical points control her choice. Her dresses must be *photogenique*; and they must not date too soon. Then, the bodices of her evening dresses must be firm enough to support the weight of the orders she wears. Again, when she is driving in a State carriage, she knows that every member of the crowd who has come to cheer her hopes to see her face. She is therefore careful to choose an upturned or small, revealing hat.

There is no doubt about it, Queen Elizabeth dresses well. She has a supreme sense of what is fit for her position, and chooses clothes eloquent of her royal life.

From ROCK & ROYALTY Sarah Mower 1987

In the 1980s there have been no livelier indicators, no more vigorous influences on British fashion than the young Royals and our multifarious pop groups. At first sight, it's a distinctly odd coupling, but viewed from an objective foreign standpoint, it becomes quite clear. For the New York teenager, the European or Japanese housewife, British fashion means pop video on MTV and splashy Di and Fergie cover stories in weekly magazines. To the world at large, our style is that which is worn by youth at its class extremes: British fashion in international markets *is* Rock 'n' Royalty...

The Princess of Wales has dared buck the old-established Royal rule that fashion is mildly suspect and should be avoided wherever possible. Queen Victoria's remark, 'Fashionable dressing – anything but that' has echoed sternly down the generations and until very recently it has been family policy always to appear suitable, but never glamorous. The Queen, distancing herself from an unseemly concern for clothes, calls her wardrobe 'my props', implying that is it the substance of her 'act', rather than her costume, that she considers to be the point.

The moment Diana stepped out of that limousine at the Goldsmiths' Hall for her first public engagement in 1981, it was obvious the focus was to shift. The Sunday Mirror breathlessly announced that her off-the-shoulder, plunging, black taffeta ballgown by the Emanuels 'would go down in history': looking back, so it has. It was the future Princess's announcement to the world that she *did* care about glamour and how she looked, that she was determined to cut a figure nobody could ignore...

While the Princess of Wales's wedding-dress is obvious as her most copied garment, with immediate impact on the mass market, her influence has been apparent, more subtly, in her own circle. In 1981 Collingwood's, the jewellers, reported a rush to the vaults to disinter the family pearls. Diana's mother, Mrs Shand-Kydd, and her sister, Lady Jane Fellowes, Princess Michael of Kent, the Duchess of Gloucester and other aristocratic ladies were soon photographed wearing similar pieces. As the Princess has hit her stride, dressing ever more sensationally, even her once resolutely uninterested in-laws have been noted taking small cues from her...

YOUNG STYLE

Above Lady Elizabeth Bowes-Lyon, now Queen Elizabeth the Queen Mother, as a debutante *1920*
Opposite Prince Edward, the Queen's youngest son,
in a twenty-first birthday photograph *1985 Tim Graham*
Overleaf: Left Princess Margaret, a twenty-first birthday portrait *1951 Beaton*
Right Princess Anne, aged almost twenty *1970 Snowdon*

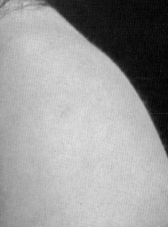

Above Lady Helen Windsor, daughter of the Duke and Duchess of Kent *1982 Snowdon*
Opposite Lady Sarah Armstrong-Jones, daughter
of Princess Margaret, photographed by her father *1981 Snowdon*

CEREMONIAL STYLE
Above Queen Mary, consort of King George V: unchanging,
statuesque, in pearls, diamond tiara and the azure Garter sash
1922 W & D Downey
Above right Queen Alexandra, consort of King Edward VII: *Vogue*
described her as 'the wonder of the world because of her remarkable
appearance of youth' *1914 W & D Downey*
Opposite The Duchess of Kent, in Court dress *1953 Beaton*

TIARA FASHION
Above Queen Elizabeth *1949 Beaton*
Below left The present Duchess of Gloucester *1984 John Swannell*
Below right Princess Alexandra *1967 Beaton*
Opposite Queen Elizabeth II *1952 Karsh*

QUEEN MARY'S STYLE
'The epitome of pure style and the antithesis of fashion' was *Vogue*'s description of Queen Mary's timeless mode of dress
Above Queen Mary with the Queen of the Belgians *1915*
Left On a hospital visit *1923*
Right Afternoon dress *1938*
Opposite Unchanged, in a quarter of a century, 'Mary R' *1939*

THE QUEEN MOTHER'S STYLE
Her signature: 'very soft, very appropriate,
unmistakably Royal clothes'
Above left Queen Elizabeth *1959*
Above right At a wartime charity display
of antique lace *1941 Beaton*
Left Timeless evening dress, at Covent
Garden *1980*, recalling *right* Hartnell's
design *1938*
Opposite The Winterhalter Queen *1939*
Beaton

THE QUEEN'S STYLE
Above In regal and ceremonial beauty, the young Queen on her accession *1952 Dorothy Wilding*
Opposite Princess Elizabeth in furs, jewels, and evening dress
at a Guildhall banquet *1950 LNA*

179

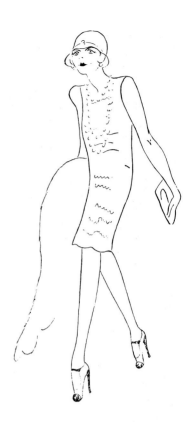

THE PATTERN OF CHIC
Left Lady Louis Mountbatten, at
Deauville *1924*
Right Cecil Beaton admired her
'completely modern behaviour',
citing 'her chic, her taut toes . . . her
sagging stance' *1927 Beaton*
Below The young hostess *1926 Maurice
Beck and Macgregor*
Opposite Lady Louis Mountbatten,
the former Edwina Ashley *1925
Hugh Cecil*

CLASSIC PRINCESS
Above The beautiful Duchess of Kent, in 'a dress of shirred net,
the bouffant skirt stiffened with horsehair' *1937 Beaton*
Opposite In classical draperies, by Molyneux *1934 Horst*

Left 'The rare beauty of Marina'
1939 Beaton
Right In state dress *1939*
Below and opposite In furs
from her trousseau *1934 Horst*

THE PRINCESS OF WALES
Above left Lady Diana Spencer, in decolleté black taffeta, by the Emanuels *1981*
Above right The Princess of Wales, in dinner jacket for a rock concert *1984 Tim Graham*

Above left In coat and hat, for a Bristol visit *1984 Cherrault*
Above right In Rifat Ozbek silk suit, for the British Fashion Show in Madrid *1987 Tim Anderson*

Above King George V in tweeds *1913*
Below left The Duke of Edinburgh in tails *1957*
Below right Prince Charles in dinner jacket *1981*
Opposite King George VI *1937*

Above The Duke of Kent *1933 Beaton*
Opposite His son-in-law the Hon Angus Ogilvy, husband
of Princess Alexandra *1967 Beaton*

GOLDEN AGE
Above Princess Marie Louise, granddaughter of Queen Victoria:
'Her memory is a golden thread that leads back to the 1870s...'
1956 Beaton
Opposite Princess Alice, Countess of Athlone, also a granddaughter
of Queen Victoria, at ninety-five *1978 Snowdon*

Above Lady Helen Windsor *1987 Glenn Harvey*
Opposite The Princess of Wales dressed by Bruce Oldfield
1987 Rex Features
Preceding pages
194 The Queen *1957 Eric*
195 Princess Margaret *1965 Beaton*
196 The Princess of Wales *1983 Cherrault*
197 Princess Margaret *1984 Snowdon*
198 The Queen Mother *1975 Parkinson*
199 The Princess of Wales *1982 Cherrault*

Overleaf
Buckingham Palace *1977 Camera Press*

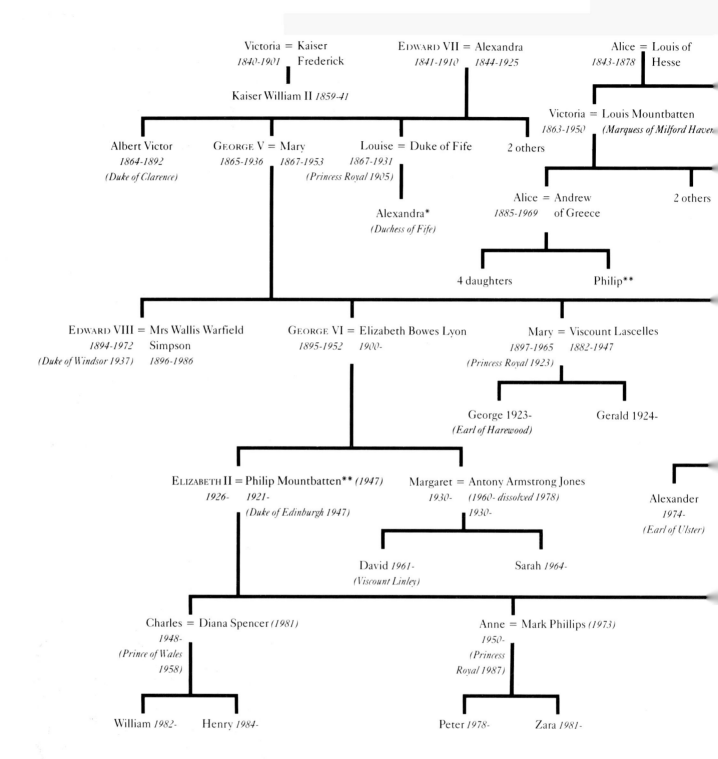

VICTORIA = Albert of Saxe - Coburg
1819-1901

Victoria = Kaiser
1840-1901 Frederick

Kaiser William II *1859-41*

EDWARD VII = Alexandra
1841-1910   *1844-1925*

Alice = Louis of
1843-1878 Hesse

Victoria = Louis Mountbatten
1863-1950 *(Marquess of Milford Haven*

Albert Victor
1864-1892
(Duke of Clarence)

GEORGE V = Mary
1865-1936 *1867-1953*

Louise = Duke of Fife
1867-1931

(Princess Royal 1905)

2 others

Alexandra*
(Duchess of Fife)

Alice = Andrew
1885-1969 of Greece

2 others

4 daughters

Philip**

EDWARD VIII = Mrs Wallis Warfield
1894-1972 Simpson
(Duke of Windsor 1937) *1896-1986*

GEORGE VI = Elizabeth Bowes Lyon
1895-1952 *1900-*

Mary = Viscount Lascelles
1897-1965 *1882-1947*

(Princess Royal 1923)

George 1923-
(Earl of Harewood)

Gerald 1924-

ELIZABETH II = Philip Mountbatten** *(1947)*
1926-   *1921-*
(Duke of Edinburgh 1947)

Margaret = Antony Armstrong Jones
1930- *(1960- dissolved 1978)*
1930-

Alexander
1974-
(Earl of Ulster)

David *1961-*
(Viscount Linley)

Sarah *1964-*

Charles = Diana Spencer *(1981)*
1948-
(Prince of Wales
1958)

Anne = Mark Phillips *(1973)*
1950-
(Princess
Royal 1987)

William *1982-*   Henry *1984-*

Peter *1978-*   Zara *1981-*

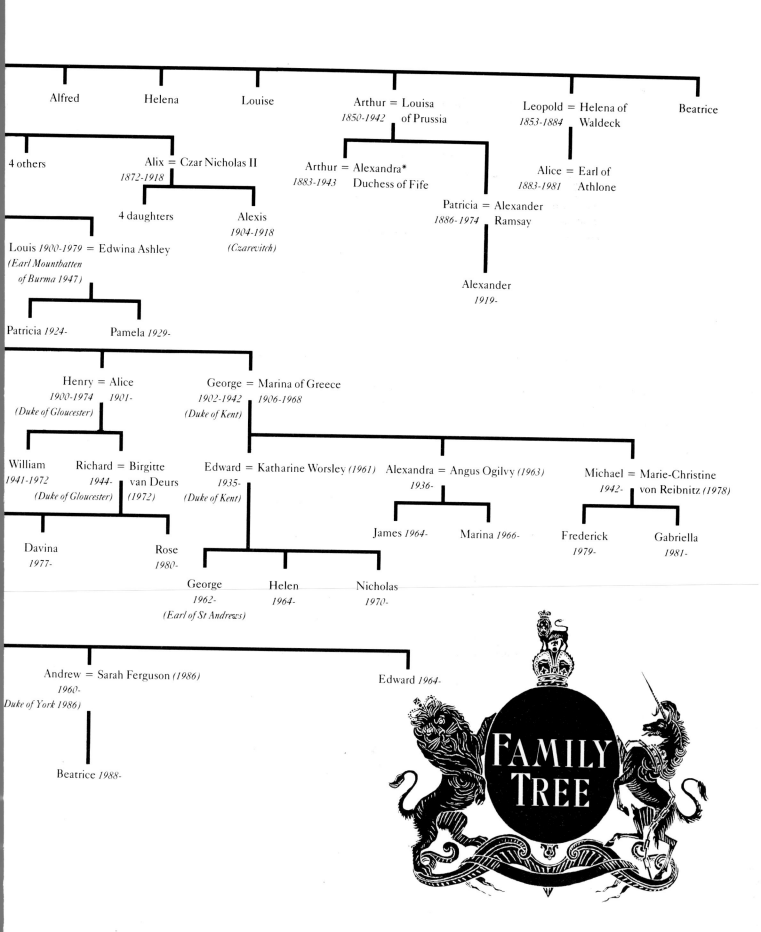

Alfred   Helena   Louise   Arthur = Louisa   Leopold = Helena of   Beatrice
1850-1942   of Prussia   *1853-1884*   Waldeck

4 others   Alix = Czar Nicholas II   Arthur = Alexandra*   Alice = Earl of
    1872-1918   *1883-1943*   Duchess of Fife   *1883-1981*   Athlone

4 daughters   Alexis   Patricia = Alexander
    1904-1918   *1886-1974*   Ramsay
    (Czarevitch)

Louis *1900-1979* = Edwina Ashley
(Earl Mountbatten
of Burma 1947)   Alexander
    1919-

Patricia *1924-*   Pamela *1929-*

Henry = Alice   George = Marina of Greece
1900-1974   *1901-*   *1902-1942*   *1906-1968*
(Duke of Gloucester)   *(Duke of Kent)*

William   Richard = Birgitte   Edward = Katharine Worsley *(1961)*   Alexandra = Angus Ogilvy *(1963)*   Michael = Marie-Christine
1941-1972   *1944-*   van Deurs   *1935-*   *1936-*   *1942-*   von Reibnitz *(1978)*
    (Duke of Gloucester)   *(1972)*   *(Duke of Kent)*

Davina   Rose   James *1964-*   Marina *1966-*   Frederick   Gabriella
1977-   *1980-*   *1979-*   *1981-*

George   Helen   Nicholas
1962-   *1964-*   *1970-*
(Earl of St Andrews)

Andrew = Sarah Ferguson *(1986)*   Edward *1964-*
1960-
Duke of York 1986)

Beatrice *1988-*

FAMILY TREE

INDEX

A

Adams, Marcus: 10
Albert, Prince: 18
Alexandra, Princess: *49, 82, 83, 155, 172*
Alexandra, Princess,
    Princess Arthur of Connaught,
    Duchess of Fife: *44, 57*
Alexandra, Queen: 7, 9, 23, 24, 42, *58,*
    136, 170
Alexis, Czarevitch: 6, 7
Alice, Princess, *see* Gloucester, Princess
    Alice, Duchess of
Alice, Princess, Countess of Athlone:
    193
Alice, Princess Andrew of Greece: 18,
    129
Amies, Hardy: *24, 24*
Anastasia, Grand Duchess 6, 7, *7*
Andrew, Prince *see* York, Prince Andrew,
    Duke of
Andrew, Prince of Greece: 18
Anne, Princess, Princess Royal: *19,* 19,
    20, 20, 22, *41,* 50, *53, 87, 93, 130, 131,*
    160, 167
Arbeid, Murray: 25
Armstrong-Jones, Lady Sarah: *152, 168*
Arthur, Duke of Connaught: 77
Arthur, Prince of Connaught: *44, 57*
Ascot: *156–7*
Ashton, Sir Frederick: *137*

B

Balmoral: 132
Bahrain, Amir of: 143
Barnardo's: 23
Birthright: 23
Blahnik, Manolo: 25
Blanch, Lesley: 15
Boucheron: 11
Bowen, Elizabeth: 19

C

Braemar, Gathering: 132, *136*
Bruson, Renato: *137*
Bryant, Arthur: 18
Buccleuch, Duke of: 11
Buck, Joan Juliet: 25
Buckingham Palace: 12, 16, 22, 25, *40,*
    43, 70, 114, *118, 202–3*

C

Caernarvon Castle: 20
Canterbury, Archbishop of: 19, 23
Cartier: 11
Charles, Prince *see* Wales, Prince
    Charles, the Prince of
Churchill, Sir Winston: 19, 23, *37*
Cierach, Lindka: 25
Ciro's: 10
Cochran, C.B.: 12
Colefax, Sybil: 11
Coward, Noël: *137*

D

Debutantes at court: 20
Decies, Lady: *6*
The Derby: 10
Devonshire, Duchess of: 27
Diana, Princess of Wales *see* Wales, the
    Princess of (Diana)
Dior: 104

E

Edelstein, Victor: 25
Edward, Prince: *41, 125, 130, 165*
Edward, Prince *see* Kent, Prince Edward,
    Duke of
Edward VII, King: 7, 9, 23
Edward VIII, King *see* Windsor, Duke of
Elizabeth II, Queen: *2,* 10, *11,* 11, 14,
    15, 16, 16, *18,* 18, *21, 22,* 22, 27, *29,*
    31, 36, 39, 40, 41, 62, 63, 70, *73, 74,*
    75, 78, 79, 80–81, 88, 89, 93, 119,
    122, 123, 124, 126–7, 131, 134, 136,
    143, 144, 147, 150, 161, 173, 178, 179,
    179, 194
Elizabeth, Queen, the Queen Mother:
    9, 9, 10, *12,* 12, *14,* 14, *15,* 15, *16,* 16,
    17, 22, 23, *24,* 24, 26, *40, 41,* 42, *45,*
    58, 70, *73, 74, 79, 88,* 114, *116, 118,*
    125, 132, 133, *136, 137, 140, 143, 152,*
    154, 162, 163, *164, 172, 176, 177, 198*
Emanuels: 23, 163
Embassy Club: 10
Eric (Carl Erickson): 11

F

Fellowes, Lady Jane: 163
Ferguson, Sarah *see* York, Duchess of
Ford, Mrs Henry II: *106*

G

Gandhi, Indira: *147*
George V, King: *6,* 6, 7, *8,* 8, 9, *12,* 12,
    13, 22, *28,* 42, *58, 155, 156–7, 188*
George VI, King: *9,* 9, *14,* 14, *15,* 15, *16,*
    19, *30,* 36, *38, 40,* 62, *73, 80–1,* 114,
    116, 118, 121, 132, 133, *136, 138, 139,*
    140, 155, 189
George, Prince *see* Kent, Prince George,
    Duke of
Glamis Castle: 9, *79*
Gloucester, Princess Alice, Duchess of:
    11, *11–12,* 12, *40, 46*
Gloucester, Duchess of (Birgitte): 163,
    172
Gloucester, Prince Henry, Duke of: *10,*
    10, 11, *30, 40, 116, 154, 159*
Gloucester, Prince Richard, Duke of: *84*
Gloucester, Prince William of: *90*
Goodwood: 10

Grenadier Guards: 119, *124*

H

Hambro, Clementine: 23, *56*
Harry, Prince, *see* Wales, Prince Harry of
Hartnell, Norman: 15, 23, *24, 24, 62*
Hendon Aerial Pageant: 10
Henry, Prince, *see* Gloucester, Prince
  Henry, Duke of
Huxley, Aldous: 9

I

Irish Guards: *125*

J

Jubilee, Silver, Elizabeth II: 22, *22, 41*
Jubilee, Silver, George V: *12*, 12, 13, 22,
  24

K

Kaiser, William II: 7, *8*, 58
Kaiserin, Augusta Victoria: *58*
Kent, Prince Edward, Duke of: *82*
Kent, Prince George, Duke of: *10*, 10,
  11, 11, *30*, 71, *82, 116, 120, 191*
Kent, Duchess of (Katharine): *137, 143*
Kent, Princess Marina, Duchess of: *11*,
  11, 12, 16, 24, *47, 61*, 71, *82, 116, 171,
  182, 183, 184, 185*
Kent, Prince Michael of: *69*
Kent, Princess Michael of: *69*, 163

L

Lascelles, George (Earl of Harewood):
  77
Lascelles, the Hon Gerald: 77
Lascelles, Henry, Viscount: 8, 10, *59*
Lebrun, President and Mme: *139*
Leslie, Seymour: 14
Louise, Princess, Princess Royal: *134*

M

Mainbocher: 15, 100
Margaret Rose, Princess: 10, *11, 16*, 16,
  20, 20, 22, *40, 48, 64*, 70, *79, 80–81,
  136, 137, 140, 153, 166, 195, 197*
Marie Louise, Princess: *192*
Marina, Princess *see* Kent, Princess
  Marina, Duchess of
Mary, Princess, Princess Royal: 8, *9*, 10,
  42, 52, 57, 59, 60, 77, *116, 128, 155*
Mary, Queen: 6–7, 8, *9, 9*, 10, *12*, 12,

16, 24, *28, 40, 42, 58, 75, 128, 135,
  156–7, 170, 174, 175*
Maugham, Syrie: 11
Maurois, André: 114
McMullin, John: 13, 24
Michael, Prince *see* Kent, Prince Michael
  of
Michael, Princess *see* Kent, Princess
  Michael of
Molyneux: 11, 61, *182*
Montagu-Douglas-Scott, Alice: *see*
  Gloucester, Princess Alice, Duchess of
Mountbatten, Lady Louis (Edwina): *10*,
  10, 16, *68*, 115, *117, 180, 181*
Mountbatten, Lord Louis: *10*, 10, 18,
  20, 20, *41*, 68, 115, *117, 142, 146*
Mountbatten, Pamela: *117*
Mountbatten, Patricia: *117*

N

Nast, Condé: 6, 7, 11, 25
Nicholas II, Czar: 7, *8*
Norfolk, Duke of: 19, 26

O

Ogilvy, Hon Angus: *49, 83, 190*
Ogilvy, James: *83*
Ogilvy, Marina: *83*
Oldfield, Bruce: *25, 25, 201*
Order of the Garter: 20, 26, 39
Ozbek, Rifat: *25, 187*

P

Parliament, State Opening: 7, 20, *29*
Patricia, Princess of Connaught: *8, 8, 44,
  72, 76*
Philip, Prince, Duke of Edinburgh: *18*,
  18, *29, 37, 41, 63, 92, 123, 126–7,
  142, 143, 150, 158, 159, 188*
Phillips, Capt Mark: 20, 22, *41, 50*
Phillips, Peter: *87, 92*
Phillips, Zara: *92*
Pollen, Arabella: 25

R

Ramsay, Alexander: *72, 76*
Ramsay, Hon Alexander: 8, *76*
Ramsay, Lady Victoria *see* Patricia,
  Princess of Connaught
Reagan, Nancy: *142, 143*
Reagan, President Ronald: *142*
Rhodes, Zandra: 22
Richard, Prince, *see* Gloucester, Prince
  Richard, Duke of
Rogers, Mr & Mrs Herman: *106*

Rowse, A.L.: 18

S

St Paul's Cathedral: 12, *22*
Schiaparelli, Elsa: 12
Shand-Kydd, Frances: 163
Simpson, Ernest: 13
Simpson, Wallis *see* Windsor, Duchess of
Sitwell, Osbert: 9
Sitwell, Sacheverell: 14
Snowdon, Lord: *20, 20, 22, 23, 64*
Spencer, Earl: 22
Strathmore, Earl of: 9
Strong, Sir Roy: 20, 22
Stuyvesant Fish, Mrs: 6

T

Thomas, Ian: 24
Trooping the Colour: 20, *31*

V

Vanderbilt, Cornelius: 6
Victoria, Queen: 6, 8, 18, 23, 24, 70, 163

W

Wales, Prince Charles, the Prince of: *2*,
  18, *19*, 19, 20. *23*, 23, 24, *51, 66–67,
  89, 125, 136, 142, 146, 149, 151, 159,
  188*
Wales, the Princess of (Diana): 22, *23,
  23*, 24, *25, 25, 54, 66–67, 86, 124,
  130, 136, 142, 145, 148, 149, 151, 152,
  163, 186, 187, 196, 199, 200*
Wales, Prince Harry of: *86, 149*
Wales, Prince William of: 24, *91, 149*
Walker, Catherine: 25
Westminster Abbey: 8, 18, 19, 25, 26
William, Prince, *see* Gloucester, Prince
  William of
Windsor, Duke of: 6, 10, *10*, 13, 14, 15,
  15, 94, 95, *96, 97, 99, 101, 102, 103,
  106, 108, 113*
Windsor, Duchess of: *13*, 13, 14, *15*, 15,
  94, 95, *98, 100, 101, 102, 103, 104,
  105, 106, 107, 110, 111, 113*
Windsor, Lady Helen: *85, 152, 169, 201*
Windsor Castle: 16, 22, *50, 62, 88*

Y

York, Prince Andrew, Duke of: 25, *41,
  43, 125, 126–7*
York, Duchess of, (Sarah): 25, *43, 55*,
  163

ACKNOWLEDGEMENTS

I have had a great deal of help in the preparation of this book. In particular, I should like to thank Alex Kroll, of Condé Nast Books, for his constant guidance and support. Kirsty Gunn and Susie Meekin researched with skill and patience; the Condé Nast Librarians, Jane Meekin and Fiona Shearer, provided endless assistance; and Robin Muir's specialist photographic knowledge was invaluable. Elizabeth Edwards laid out the Family Tree; and Sara Longworth helped in numerous ways.

Others at Condé Nast to whom I am indebted include Lillie Davies and Elaine Shaw, who oversaw the editorial and photographic business; and Terry Boxall and Barbara Marcan, who skilfully worked on the technical side. My grateful thanks are also due to Bunny Cantor and Max Steiger; Dudley Mountney, Sudhir Pithwa and Chris Clark; and to Caroline Curtis and Richard Holmes.

Finally, I should like to acknowledge the work of the successive *Vogue* Editors who commissioned and published the material in this book, and the great photographers, artists and writers who created it.